Strategies For Successfully Buying Or Selling A Business

Russell L. Brown

THE BUSINESS BOOK PRESS
RDS ASSOCIATES, INC.
41Brainerd Road
Niantic, Connecticut 06357
Tel. (860) 691-0081 / Fax: (860) 691-1145
E-mail: rds@businessbookpress.com
Internet: www.BusinessBookPress.com

Strategies For Successfully Buying Or Selling A Business

Copyright 2002, Russell L. Brown

The complete guide to buying or selling a business; everything buyers and sellers need to know to find each other, negotiate, and successfully close the deal.

Published by The Business Book Press, a division of RDS Associates, Inc., 41Brainerd Road, Niantic, Connecticut 06357. This book is a second edition.

Publisher's Cataloging-in-Publication
(Provided by Quality Books, Inc.)

Brown, Russell Lee.
    Strategies for successfully buying or selling a business /
Russell L. Brown. --2nd ed.
    224p. cm.
    Includes index.
    ISBN: 0-96574004-8

    1. Sale of business enterprises.   2. Business enterprises--
Purchasing. 3. Real estate business.   I. Title.

    HD1393.25.B76 1997   658.1`6
                            QBI97-40644

Foreword

This book provides practical guidance and key insider information for potential buyers and sellers of small to medium-sized profitable operating businesses in the United States. It will help buyers and sellers of businesses find each other, determine a fair market value for the business, conduct productive negotiations, and successfully close the deal. By using the principles, ideas, hints, insider's secrets, and experiences described in this book, the buyer and seller will be able to save themselves significant amounts of time, aggravation, and money as they move forward with their transaction.

Some sections of the book are directed more at sellers than buyers, and vice versa, but it's strongly recommended that you read all sections because you'll find useful information from both perspectives in all sections. For example, it will be highly useful for a seller to understand how a buyer is being advised to find a profitable business for sale and it will be equally valuable for a buyer to learn how sellers are being told to position their businesses for sale. Both parties will benefit by knowing how the other will approach this complex transaction of buying and selling a business.

Even if the business owner already has a successor in mind such as a child, sibling, trusted employee, etc., this book will help the business owner to establish a value for the business and will provide a framework to work within for transferring ownership.

For the purposes of this book, small to medium sized businesses are defined as those businesses that have one to one hundred employees and up to ten million dollars in annual sales. These are very arbitrary ranges and should only be used as a broad guide. However, this book recognizes that the vast majority of businesses sold every day have fewer than twenty five employees and less than a million dollars in annual sales, and emphasis has been placed on the buying and selling of businesses in this category. Many of the fundamentals presented in this book are equally true for the Main Street retail store or service business, as well as for a Fortune 500 company. The principles are the same, just the level and amount of detail differs. Everyone involved in the buying and selling of a business will find this book extremely useful and informative.

I have presented information that is as accurate and current as possible. However, due to the varied nature of the laws of our different states, constantly changing resource addresses, the great diversity between each business situation, and based on using plain good old common sense, the reader is cautioned to independently verify all information before engaging in any business transaction.

Good luck with your objectives, and I'm pleased to be able to assist you through what could be one of the most challenging and rewarding undertakings in your business life!

Russell L. Brown
Author

Introduction

So, you want to buy or sell a business! Personally, I'd much rather collect venom on a rattlesnake farm; but then, I've been a business broker for many years. Actually, many transactions of this nature take place every day and there are ways to avoid most of the many traps and pitfalls involved. However, it will almost never be easy!

I've written this book for the specific purpose of alerting you to potential real life issues and problems that may occur in the process of buying or selling a small or medium-sized business and to provide ideas on how to solve them. All of the accounts are based on my and my contemporaries' experiences as business brokers, i.e., crazy people who try to act as middlemen between buyers and sellers of businesses! I've included some very practical and useful information regarding basic business concepts and financial issues which you'll need to know when buying or selling a business. I've also tried to make sure that this book is not a high level tutorial that you'd need to be an accountant or a lawyer to understand.

This book is not about starting up a new business, multi-level marketing (MLM), or buying a new franchise. These forms of business enterprise are unique unto themselves and information about them can be found in other publications. Additionally, there are many more books, reports, pamphlets, etc. that deal with these and other subjects relating to buying, selling, or determining the value of an operating business that are available through the publishers of this book which you'll find useful.

I've organized this book in a logical sequence that will most likely correspond to your actual experience as you pursue the purchase or sale of a business. I've started with a discussion of the business broker because for most buyers and sellers this is the first person that you'll deal with. Next, I cover the topic of valuing the business because this is a key piece of information that everyone needs to know as soon as possible. I follow this with chapters devoted to buyers and sellers efficiently and effectively finding each other and then move into the next logical area; negotiations. I wind things up with chapters about closing the deal to buy the business and post-sale issues. I've chosen to introduce and explain various business concepts that you'll need to know as they arise within the chapters and sections. This will simplify your understanding of these important points.

I have also included a fairly extensive glossary of terms common to the purchase and sale of an operating business. I recommend that you refer to the glossary whenever you come across a term that you're not familiar with and include it as part of your overall reading of this book. I've minimized the jargon that you don't really need to know and put things in common sense everyday language wherever possible. The glossary also contains some terms not specifically referred to in the main body of the book, but which you may find useful as you pursue the purchase or sale of a business.

I've also included as appendices some examples of various business purchase and sale documents that you'll need to become familiar with as you buy or sell a business. However, these documents are examples only for the purpose of illustrating the kinds of legal forms necessary in this process. These in no way should take the place of legal, accounting, or other professional services specific to your particular needs. If legal advice or other expert assistance is required, the services of a competent professional person should be sought.

You should also be aware that special laws exist regarding the structuring and sale of a limited partnership, tax shelter situation, or other complex business structure. However, these are very specialized forms of business purchase and sale which will probably not involve you and are beyond the scope of this book. This book addresses the tens of thousands of other transactions that occur each year involving relatively "straightforward" sales of privately owned and operated small and medium sized businesses on Main Street, USA (which has unfortunately for many small town centers increasingly come to mean a mega-mall).

What I will do in this book is prepare you for the actualities of "real life." I have included facts, information, ideas, hints, strategies and guidelines that you'll probably not find anywhere else. They will most likely prove invaluable as buyers and sellers attempt to deal with each other — whether through a business broker or on their own. Also, business brokers will find the information provided here a rich source of ideas about how to improve their existing services and consequently, expand their sales and commission.

The last appendix in this book is a Reader Feedback Request where I ask for your comments about how useful this book is to you. I'd like to know what your thoughts are, and I'd very much like to hear from you.

Table of Contents

**To The Business Owners And
Potential Business Owners
Of The World . . .**

*"Far better it is to dare mighty things, to win glorious
triumphs, even though checkered by failure, than to
rank with those poor spirits who neither enjoy much
nor suffer much, because they live in the great twilight
that knows neither victory nor defeat"*

Theodore Roosevelt
1899

1

The Business Broker

- *Difficulties In Selling A Business Without A Broker*
- *The Fair Deal Versus The Best Deal*
- *Rules Governing Business Brokers*
- *Finding A Good Business Broker*
- *Key Questions To Ask A Business Broker*
- *Listing Agreements*
  - *Open Agency Listing*
  - *Exclusive Agency Listing*
  - *Exclusive Right To Sell Listing*
- *Facts And Figures*

I'll start off by explaining what a business broker's role is, because most buyers and sellers of businesses use the services of a business broker. Keep in mind that if you don't use a broker, then you as a buyer or seller, will have to be involved much more intimately in the hundreds of details of the transaction which will take a great deal of your time. However, as a seller you can potentially save the costs associated with a broker's typical commission of 6–10% of the total business selling price. As I'll explain later, this may not be a wise move if you really want to sell your business for a fair price in a reasonable time frame. However, you'll want to read this chapter carefully whether you use a broker or not. Unfortunately, some business brokers are not fully familiar with some of the concepts in this book and accordingly, it will help your position by being more knowledgeable than they are. If you don't use a business broker, then you are effectively operating in that capacity yourself and if you're like me, you'll want every piece of information possible to improve your chances of success.

The business broker acts primarily as a fiduciary agent (position of trust) for business owners in an attempt to sell their businesses through sales efforts to individuals or for acquisition by other firms. Buyers should never forget that in most cases, the broker works for the seller. This puts the broker in a naturally adversarial role relative to the buyers. The broker will most likely be extremely helpful to both the buyer and seller during the purchase and sale process but the broker is not on the buyer's side! However, in almost all cases, a broker doesn't earn a commission until a sale is completed, so in reality, the broker is very interested in seeing that a closing takes place. Buyers and sellers should always keep this fact in mind and deal with the broker accordingly.

Difficulties In Selling A Business Without A Broker

Some business owners attempt to sell their businesses themselves, and they soon find that the sale of a business is prohibitively difficult to accomplish without a broker (or someone) acting as an intermediary for many of the following reasons:

- The seller often doesn't know how to properly value the business.

- The seller often doesn't know how to present the business in its best light from a buyer's perspective.

- The seller is usually unable to efficiently attract qualified buyers to the business and at the same time maintain confidentiality that the business is for sale from employees, customers, and competitors.

- The seller is frequently unable to judge a buyer's seriousness; much time can be wasted by sellers dealing with "lookers." Many potential buyers are victims of wishful thinking and they don't have the financial or intestinal ability to complete the deal.

- The seller is unable to create a competitive atmosphere among potential buyers.

- The seller sometimes doesn't know how to evaluate offers as to their full value or how to financially structure the business sale to make the business as attractive as possible to a potential buyer.

- The buyer basically doesn't trust the seller or the information provided (and rightly so in many cases!).

- The buyer's and seller's interests tend to polarize along rigid, opposing lines. They are natural adversaries, and there is no middleman to propose compromise.

- The buyer and seller generally don't know how to arrange financing for the buyer or arrange payout security for the seller.

- The buyer and seller almost always don't know how to bring a transaction to a closing.

Many sellers recognize the problems of attempting to sell their business without a competent broker, and as a result they look for help. The friendly neighborhood real estate agent is always ready to take a listing for a business. It may soon become apparent to the seller that the agent may know something about listing residential or even commercial real estate, but has very little knowledge about the workings of a business and doesn't have the unique skills and information needed to properly represent an operating business for sale. The resulting competency void can be best filled by a professional business broker. Beware of the real estate agent who doesn't know the difference between the sales revenue, the accounts receivable, and the reconstructed Income and Expense Statement!

The Fair Deal Versus The Best Deal

Other professionals who can and often do act as intermediaries in the purchase and sale of a business are lawyers and accountants. This brings me to my first of fifteen laws of the business buying and selling jungle:

Strategic Jungle Law #1:

"Lawyers are deal killers!"

There certainly is an important role for a competent commercial law attorney to advise and prepare the legal structure of a business purchase and sale transaction. The problem arises when lawyers see themselves as business negotiators out to get the "best deal" for their clients. They frequently forget that the "best deal" has to involve both parties, the buyer and seller, and that compromise is usually the only solution. Lawyers generally have a very difficult time with compromise relative to their client because they see their role as advising their clients on how to get the better deal. This doesn't always work because the buyer's lawyer may be pushing their client towards the "best deal" as well. In general, to successfully buy and sell a business, the "fair deal" versus the "best deal" has to be reached so that both the buyer and the seller are satisfied. Unless you remember that lawyers and accountants are only advisors and may not have any better insight into the business deal than you do, you may end up in a situation where you'll never be able to buy or sell a business.

Rules Governing Business Brokers

Many states and other governmental agencies have laws dealing with the activities of business brokers, but in general the field is not tightly regulated which can prove to be a problem for business buyers and sellers. On one hand, it's relatively simple for a qualified business broker to "open for business." On the other hand, this makes it easy for anyone else, qualified or not, to enter the profession. In some areas of the country, this tends to create a clutter of unqualified individuals who will provide a disservice to everyone involved. These unqualified brokers tend to create a negative impression in the business community as to the general competency level of all business brokers. Later in this chapter, I'll give you some ideas about how to find a good business broker.

Because whatever laws exist involving the conduct of business brokers are specific to a particular state, this book can't be fully definitive for your particular situation. I suggest that first time buyers and sellers may want to contact their own Secretary of State and Real Estate Commission to determine just what laws will apply and consequently what protection they can expect. In general, in any business sale involving the transfer of real estate (note that business assets other than real estate are personal property), state laws will require a business broker to have a real estate agent's license from the state in which they are doing business. However, most business sales do not involve transfer of title to real estate (which includes leases of real property) and therefore, are not under the related laws which tend to provide some protection to the public from unscrupulous individuals. If you are a seller listing your business for sale and it also involves the sale of related real estate, make sure that the business broker representing you has a real estate license.

Finding A Good
Business Broker

As a matter of basic principle, all business brokers dealing with the public are bound to be honest and forthright in their conduct concerning the businesses that they represent for sale. They also have a fiduciary relationship (position of trust) to uphold between themselves and their clients (the business seller, in most cases). They must present a business for sale in its "best light" without misrepresenting any facts. This is what automatically sets up an adversarial relationship with the buyer. At times, you'll find that a broker's obligation as a fiduciary to the seller may appear to be at odds with their required conduct with prospective buyers. Never forget the next law of the jungle, which also tends to be the most basic of the laws:

Strategic Jungle Law #2:

"Caveat businessus emptor!"
(let the business buyer beware!)

Sometimes buyers hire business brokers to represent them in finding and buying a business for sale. I don't have any hard facts about how often this happens, but I believe that it's very rare. Generally, a good business broker won't represent a potential buyer on a contingency basis because of the well known fact among brokers that the vast majority of potential business buyers never actually buy a business. However, if a serious buyer can find a good professional business broker to represent them on a fixed fee (or hourly rate) basis, it may be well worth their money. Having a seasoned professional on the buyer's side could mean a lower purchase price, and a more successfully financially structured deal that may ultimately help to ensure that the business buyer succeeds with the newly acquired business.

While still unusual, there is an increasing trend in business brokerage towards the use of transaction brokers. These are business brokers or more usually acquisition and merger specialists who basically represent both sides in the transaction. They act as facilitators to the business deal and are bound by fiduciary responsibilities to equally represent both sides; the buyer and the seller. Their principal value is to act as facilitators, intermediaries, and problem solvers. They're paid a commission from both the buyer and the seller upon closing, but there's almost always a negotiated fee paid in advance in case the transaction never completes. In general, transaction brokers are not involved in the purchase and sale of a small business but rather are involved in a large acquisition or merger in the multi-million dollar range.

In case you're wondering what the difference is between a merger and an acquisition; a merger is when one company takes over another company and only one company survives, and an acquisition is when one company buys another company but that company survives as a subsidiary or other type of semi-autonomous entity.

Once you've decided to retain the services of a professional business broker you'll need to find someone suitable for your specific situation. The landscape is filled with highly professional and competent brokers as well as many "wannabe's." A good place to start to find a qualified business broker is with the International Business Brokers Association (IBBA):

IBBA Headquarters
401 North Michigan Avenue, Suite 2200
Chicago, Illinois 60611-4267
888-686-IBBA (4222)   312-673-6599 (fax)
E-mail: admin@ibba.org

Key Questions To Ask
A Business Broker

Because selling your business will probably be one of the four or five most important events in your life, you owe it to yourself and all you've worked for to get the best possible assistance with this complex transaction. How do you ensure that you get the right person to represent you and your business for sale? Well, as a start, before you list your business for sale with a broker, you should ask them the following crucial questions and make a selection decision based on your satisfaction with their answers:

- **How Many Businesses Have You Successfully Brokered in the Past Year?** This is a very important question to ask the business broker, but you have to carefully evaluate the answer. What you want to find out is how active the broker is in marketing and closing the sale of businesses. Because some business transactions involve very large dollar amounts and are very complicated, a good business broker may only handle two or three actual closings per year. On the other hand, if the broker is primarily representing small "Mom and Pop" operations that sell in the $100,000 range, then you should expect that the broker will handle about 10 to 15 closings annually. Many general business brokers will in fact have a range of closings from $50,000 on up to an occasional $500,000+ sale. In general, business brokers who close deals in the one million to five million dollar range are considered "middle-market" brokers. Those who operate in the rarefied air of the five million dollar plus range are generally referred to as mergers and acquisitions specialists because most deals in these upper price ranges involve the sale of the business to another company. What you're looking to learn with this question is to not only find out how active the business broker is, but how successful. Although there aren't any reliable statistics that you can compare a business broker to, you should look for a success ratio of about one to five, or better. This means that a broker sells one business out of every five businesses listed. The trouble with this statistic is that it doesn't take into consideration the brokers who accept many marginal listings to "have them on the shelf", yet still manage to sell a good number overall. It also doesn't consider the multi-broker office and co-listings which can skew a broker's apparent performance one way or another. The best that you can do with this question is to satisfy yourself that the broker is apparently actively taking listings and routinely closing deals.

- **What Types of Businesses Have You Successfully Represented for Sale?** It's very important that the business broker you retain to represent your business for sale is somewhat familiar with the type of business you're in. Realistically, it isn't absolutely necessary that a broker has actually sold a business exactly like yours, but you should look for someone who is at least familiar with your industry. You'll find it much easier to explain your business operations to the broker and they in turn will be much more able to represent your business for sale in its best light.

If the business broker is familiar with your specific type of business or its industry, they'll know the business jargon, sales trends, projected growth rates, and other information important to communicating with you and knowledgeable prospective buyers.

You may want to select a business broker who specializes in your particular type of business. I've listed some examples of specialties here so you can have an idea of the range and breadth of specialization that you'll find.

- Restaurants
- Franchise Re-sales
- Manufacturing
- Re-locatable Businesses

- Vending Routes
- Professional Practices
- Country Stores
- Marinas
- Bed & Breakfast Inns
- Hotels and Motels
- Self-Storage Facilities

- **What's the Range of Business Valuations That You Have Successfully Brokered?** This question is similar to the first one except that you need to try to find out which portion of the general business market the broker is most active in. If you expect your business to sell for a million plus dollars, then perhaps the broker who's never brokered a deal over $150,000 wouldn't be right for you. On the other hand, you may not want to hire the multi-million dollar mergers and acquisitions specialist to represent your one-location retail store that you expect to sell for about $100,000. It could be that your situation won't get the attention that it deserves from the broker because of its relatively small size. Due to the complexity of most business sales, even the small ones, it's usually better that you retain a business broker who is working towards the high end of their range than one who is working towards the lower end. You most likely won't suffer from a lack of expertise, but you'll gain a much more interested broker. Don't forget that most business brokers work on a contingency fee basis with their fee dependent not only on a successful sale, but also on the size of the sale. A broker may work extra hard to close a deal at the higher end of their normal range because the incentive is the greatest.

- **What Advertising Methods Do You Use to Find a Buyer for My Business?** Advertising methods are important to the successful sale of a business, but not crucial. Many experienced business brokers have a substantial backlog of potential buyers to whom they can present your business without ever having to expose your business to the general marketplace. Additionally, most business brokers have extensive business community contacts they can use to discreetly seek a potential buyer without having to advertise. However, many businesses must be marketed in a broader venue and it's in your best interests to learn what advertising methods the broker intends to use for your business. Many professional business brokers will present you with their marketing plan for your business and seek your input about ways to enhance their proposed approach. Some of the advertising methods a business broker might use are:
  - newspaper classified ads
  - magazine classified ads

- broker agency newsletter to other brokers, as well as potential buyers
- classified ads in national periodicals specifically selling businesses
- advertising on the Internet

This last item has become extremely effective. It's always been a tremendous challenge for buyers, sellers, and brokers of small businesses to efficiently find each other and close the deal. Many would-be business buyers are willing to relocate anywhere in the country for the right business. Many businesses themselves are not geographic specific and can be relocated to the buyer's area. Business brokers have many times found themselves in the position of having a motivated and financially capable buyer wanting to buy a particular type of business, but they've been unable to locate the right situation for the buyer. Similarly, business brokers sometimes find themselves with a high quality business for sale but have difficulty finding the right buyer for the business within their immediate geographic area.

At any given point in time there are approximately 850,000 small to medium sized businesses for sale in the United States. Concurrently, many brokers estimate that they have at least five qualified buyers for every business they have for sale. This means that there are over 4,000,000 buyers spread across the country from Maine to Hawaii right now looking for a business to buy! The logistics of matching the right business with the right buyer has up until the advent of the Internet been overwhelming when you consider these numbers. The traditional method of print media advertising is cumbersome, not especially effective, very expensive, and is extremely inefficient. These problems are all fast coming to an end through the use of the Internet by business brokers!

As a business seller, you should closely question the business broker about how they intend to use the Internet to find a qualified buyer for your business. Does the broker have his own Web site? Do they know the best commercial sites to discreetly advertise your business for sale? Any good marketing plan for the sale of your business should include an Internet strategy or you may not be getting the best exposure for your planned business sale.

- **What Valuation Method Do You Use in Helping Me to Establish a Selling Price for My Business?** If you're going to rely on the business broker to assist you in establishing a value for your business, you'll want to find out what business valuation method they intend to use. There are dozens of variations of ways to value a business, but they can be distilled down to four fundamental methods:

- asset based valuation
- market comparison valuation
- income based valuation
- rules of thumb/industry formulas (for rough estimation purposes)

If your business is a currently operating profitable company with at least three years of history, then the income based valuation method is most likely the best approach to setting a realistic asking price. Although many business brokers have developed "rules of thumb" for arriving at a ballpark estimation for the value of a business, a business value and therefore its asking price, should usually not be based on such a crude estimate. You may want to ask the business broker to estimate the value of your business using both the market comparison valuation and an income based valuation to see if there's a significant value difference in your favor. Either way, the broker will need to rely heavily on you to provide specific details about the financial operation of your business before they use any valuation method.

You may want to seriously consider having a separate, independent business valuation done by a business appraiser. You'll have to pay separately for this and fees can typically range anywhere from $1,000 to $25,000, depending on the complexity of your business. The advantage to you is that you'll have the most confidence in the appraisal, because the appraiser has no vested interest in skewing the value one way or another. You'll be able to have a written copy of the valuation and the basis for it for your broker (or you) to use with prospective buyers.

If you rely on your listing broker to do an appraisal estimate, you most likely won't receive a copy of the appraisal. Business brokers working on a contingency basis are reluctant to release their valuation analysis to a seller because some sellers have been known to use business brokers to receive a "free" business valuation. However, you may want to ask the business broker what their policy is in this regard.

- **What Steps Do You Take to Ensure the Confidentiality Regarding My Business Being for Sale?** Many business owners are very wary of letting it be known to anyone that their business is for sale. There are many good reasons for this and the ability to maintain the confidentiality of the planned business sale is an important capability of the business broker. However, one of the hardest things to do when selling an operating business is to maintain the confidentiality of the sale. Although no reputable broker can ever guarantee complete confidentiality, there are many things they can do to maximize the chances that your business sale will remain discreet. The two most important things are:

- Using discretion in the details that are included in any advertising for your business

- Requiring legally binding documentation signed by potential buyers which requires them not to disclose any of the details they learn about your business (or even the fact that it's for sale).

Also, in an effort to maintain confidentiality, the business broker should:

- Be willing to show the premises after normal business hours.

- Be willing to pose as an insurance agent or some other professional having a legitimate benign interest in touring the business during normal hours.

- **How Will You Safeguard My Business Financial Information from Inappropriate Use?** To facilitate the process of selling your business and to allow the business broker to present your business in its best light, you'll need to provide sensitive business financial information. Eventually the business broker is going to have to actually show the physical assets and premises of the business. Every business owner naturally has a concern about the safeguarding of that information from competitors and others with no legitimate need to know. Most professional business brokers will use some sort of Confidentiality Agreement with potential buyers. A sample Confidentiality Agreement is provided as Appendix D.

  Additionally, the business broker should have a security arrangement within their office where only the listing broker controls the access to the seller's detailed financial information. No one other than the listing broker should have access to the seller's business financial information without the express consent of the listing broker. A business broker should be able to articulate this policy to a seller.

  In some cases, sellers may want to restrict access to their financial statements only through themselves or their accountants. This is less efficient than letting the business broker handle things, but it will add a measure of security to your financial information. You should ask the business broker what their policy is about this.

- **What's Your Education and Training Background?** A business broker's educational and training background is not always a good indicator of a successful brokering endeavor. Brokers come from many walks of life and hugely divergent backgrounds. In general, a broker's track record in selling businesses is much more indicative of their potential than their education and training. However, you may be able to get a feel for the broker's sophistication and sense of your business based on their education and training. Typically, a broker with an engineering background will be more successful with technology or manufacturing based companies. A broker with a Bachelor of Arts degree may be more sensitive to the nuances of a publishing company, graphic arts studio, bookstore, etc. The most important aspect of this question is to find out specifically what business education and/or training they've had. A business broker with an MBA or a CPA may have a better understanding of business fundamentals than someone without a formal business education. It's also important to determine if the broker is keeping up with the latest knowledge and approaches in the field by finding out what professional training they've taken and designations or certifications they've earned, and when. For example, business brokers may obtain advanced training from the following professional organizations:

- Institute of Business Appraisers (IBA)
  954-584-1144   www.instbusapp.org

- American Society of Appraisers
  703-478-2228   www.appraisers.org

- National Association of Certified Valuation Analysts
  801-486-0600   www.nacva.com

- International Business Brokers Association
  888-686-4222   www.ibba.org

- **What References from Satisfied Buyers and Sellers Can You Provide to Me?** All experienced brokers usually have a portfolio of testimonials, thank-you letters, and names of satisfied clients that they'll provide to a serious new prospective client. Most often these references will be from the sellers, the business broker's most usual client. Some have also represented buyers or have received positive comments from satisfied buyers on the other side of the transaction. These are all important for you to check out to satisfy yourself as to the level of satisfaction from others that the broker has worked for.

Additionally, you should ask for references from attorneys, accountants, and bankers that the broker has recently worked with in closing business deals. Most likely, the broker won't have any written testimonials from them, but you should be able to obtain several names of professionals who may be familiar or known to you from whom you can receive an unbiased opinion as to the broker's expertise in facilitating the sale of a business. These references may be of more significance to you than the testimonials of past clients. The broker most likely will only provide you with satisfied clients as references. By talking with the attorneys and CPA's involved in the broker's more recent closings, you may be able to get a broader perspective of the business broker's capabilities.

If you are dealing with an investment banker, they keep a record of their successful transactions in a written form that they refer to as "tombstones." Some business brokers and mergers & acquisition specialists may also refer to their completed deals as "tombstone" listings.

• **What Steps Do You Take to Ensure That You Introduce My Business to Qualified Buyers Only?** A qualified buyer is someone who is ready and able to buy a business such as the one being offered for sale. I've deliberately left out the second word from the real estate phrase that most of us know: ready, willing, and able. In the first exposure of a business for sale to a potential buyer, you certainly can't expect them to be willing to buy, but your broker should have a way to qualify a buyer as ready and able or you'll all potentially be wasting a lot of time.

A ready and able buyer, i.e., a qualified buyer is:

  • Someone who is honestly looking for a business to purchase.

  • Someone who has the motivation and personal commitment to purchase a business.

  • Someone who has the financial resources (or access to them) to consummate the purchase.

  • Someone who has the "right" motivations (e.g., you don't want sensitive business information being given to one of your business competitors)!

A professional business broker should know how to sort through the many non-qualified buyers to get to the few who actually do have the means and motivation to buy your business. However, once the unqualified potential buyers have been culled out, a high percentage of qualified buyers eventually do buy a business.

Many business brokers use a questionnaire such as a Buyer's Financial Qualification Statement (Appendix E) to qualify a buyer. It's usually not very easy to get this from a prospective buyer in such an early stage in the process of potentially buying the business, but a good business broker will know how. If it's determined that the buyer is not financially qualified to buy the business, a great deal of wasted time on everyone's part will be avoided. One strategy that the broker can use in asking the potential buyer to fill out the Statement is to state that it's only a reciprocal exchange of sensitive financial information between business parties; the seller provides the business IRS Tax Returns and other financial data to the buyer, and the buyer provides pertinent personal financial data about themselves to the seller.

- **Are You a Licensed Real Estate Broker?** This question is important to the business seller for several reasons:

  - You want to find out if the business broker splits their time between selling real estate and businesses or if they concentrate on selling businesses only. Usually you'll receive much better service and results if the business broker concentrates on selling businesses only.

  - Many businesses involve some sort of real estate to be transferred as part of the business. In all 50 states, a real estate license is required to represent real estate for sale. In addition to actual land and buildings, real estate laws also cover a lease for the rented premises. You'll want to make sure that the business broker either is a licensed real estate agent or has a real estate agent that they work with if your business sale will involve the transfer of any real estate, including assignments of leases.

  - In several states, it's required by law that business brokers be licensed as real estate agents whether the sale of the business involves real estate or not. These states as of this writing are:

Alaska	Idaho	South Dakota
Arizona	Illinois	Utah
California	Louisiana	Washington
District of Columbia	Michigan	Wisconsin
Oregon	Minnesota	Wyoming
Florida	Nebraska	
Georgia	Nevada	

It should be noted that Illinois also requires that a business broker doing business in the state be registered under the Illinois Security Department.

- **What Information Do You Need From Me About My Business?** To properly represent your business for sale for the best value from the widest array of qualified potential buyers, the business broker will need as much information about your business as you can reasonably provide. At a minimum, the broker should ask for:

  - Financial Statements (Profit & Loss and Balance Sheets for the last three fiscal years)

- Interim Financial Statement, (to date, for the current fiscal year)

- IRS Tax Returns, (last three years, minimum)

- Lease or Rental Agreement, including renewal options for all real estate

- Franchise Agreement, (if applicable)

- List of furniture, fixtures, equipment, including estimated "fair market value"

- Licensing, Distributorship, Manufacturing Agreements, etc.

- List of current contracts, including face amount, completion date, percentage completed

- Copies of Patents, Trade Names, Trademarks, or Copyrights

- Customer Lists

- **What Are Your Fees For Representing My Business For Sale?** Many business brokers have a standard fee that they charge which is usually 10 percent of the total value of a business sale up to some set value after which the percentage declines on some scale. Frequently, the total value includes all tangible and intangible assets, including the cash, accounts receivable, and inventory if these are conveyed as part of the business transaction. A typical fee arrangement for a business broker may look like this:

10%	of all business value up to $500,000
9%	of all business value on the next $100,000
8%	of all business value on the next $100,000
7%	of all business value on the next $100,000
6%	of all business value on the next $100,000 and
5%	on all value over $1,000,000.

You want to keep in mind that there is no standard fee structure in the industry and any quoted fees are open to negotiation between yourself and the business broker. Not only is it possible to negotiate a different fee structure, but you may want to exclude certain assets, such as accounts receivable and cash, from the application of the fee.

Other negotiating points you may want to address are the payment terms of the fee. Most business brokers want to receive their entire fee at the closing, but payout terms may be negotiated that lower the up-front cash requirements for the buyer and therefore improve the ability for you to sell your business.

In some cases, a broker will require an up-front fee be paid to represent your business for sale. The amount paid will usually be deducted from the sales commission at the time of sale. If no closing takes place the fee is not refundable. Many of the more successful and highly qualified brokers are requiring this arrangement as a way of smoothing out the vagaries of the exclusive contingency fee process. It can be argued that you'll receive more competent professional representation with this fee arrangement.

If you do pay an up-front fee as an advance against future commission, you should insist on a written appraisal of your business valuation as a quid pro quo. In the event your business doesn't sell, you'll at least have the written valuation to use in any future sales attempts.

Listing Agreements

There are basically three types of listing agreements or "authorizations to sell" that you can enter into, and depending whether you're a seller, buyer, or broker, they'll each have different importance to you.

The "**open agency listing**" gives the broker the right to sell the business, but without any specified performance requirements for either the seller or the broker. The sellers still have the right to sell the business themselves and also to enter into other open listing agreements with other brokers. The broker, in turn, doesn't have any obligation to use their best (or any) effort in marketing that business. In general, open listings are the least desirable to the broker, and they'll avoid them if possible because they'll be competing against too many others (including the seller). The broker could do a fine job with marketing a business and then lose out on a commission because some other broker (or the owner) sells the situation first. Without an exclusive right to sell, the seller has a strong competitive advantage over the broker; price. The owner can sell the business for less if there doesn't have to be a broker's commission paid. Brokers may decide to accept an open listing on a business if they feel that the price, terms, or some other conditions will make the business very hard to sell and they don't want to spend much time (or money) marketing it. Sometimes brokers will like to have the business "on the shelf" in inventory, in case they run across a buyer who would be interested in it. In general, only brokers who aren't confident that they can sell a business and don't plan to use their best marketing efforts, will take an open listing. Another case for a broker taking an open listing is if the seller will absolutely not give the broker an exclusive type of listing, and the broker feels strongly that they can sell the business. However, always remember that good brokers have a very valuable service to offer, and they should be given an exclusive listing if you really want them to work to sell the business.

The **"exclusive agency listing"** gives the broker the exclusive right to sell the business as an agency (brokerage firm). The seller retains the right to sell the business personally, but can't give a listing to any other agency during the term of the agreement. The broker is required to exert their full and best efforts to market that business. Although this isn't the most desirable type of listing for all concerned, it's many times an acceptable compromise over the open listing. In general, a seller won't be able to sell the business without the broker, and in most cases, won't even make the attempt if there's an aggressive marketing approach taken by the broker. However, the broker may be competing with the seller if the seller decides to actively pursue selling the business. The seller will have an advantage over the broker in that the business can be sold for 6 – 10% less than the broker can sell it for (the amount of the commission). In most cases, it's much more advantageous for the seller and broker to work together to accomplish a sale and any competition between them may actually be counter-productive.

The **"exclusive right to sell listing"** is the most desirable situation from the broker's point of view and in my opinion, the best arrangement for the business seller as well. Most businesses that are sold are done so under exclusive right to sell agreements. This listing gives the broker the sole and exclusive right to sell the business. Even if the present owner personally sells the business, the agreed upon commission must be paid to the broker, but this rarely happens. The marketing requirements for the broker are the same as for an exclusive agency, and they must use their best efforts to sell that business. The advantage to the broker with this listing is that they can feel much more secure in investing their time, effort, and advertising money in promoting the sale of the business without fear that the owner or anyone else will cut them out by finding another buyer. The advantage to the seller is that the best service is received from the protected and therefore, highly motivated business broker. The only potential disadvantage for this type of listing is the risk that the business seller takes relative to whether or not the broker will provide their best efforts. The seller will be unable to sell the business themselves (without owing the broker a commission) or to give the listing to another broker until the term of the listing agreement has expired. The best solution to this disadvantage is to make sure at the start that you're using a professional, reputable business broker to represent you and your business. Take the time to find a good, trustworthy business broker before you sign a listing agreement of any kind.

NOTE: Always avoid confusion if you, the seller, switch brokers. If you're changing an expiring listing agreement from one business brokerage agency to another, then make sure that the new broker provides proper notification to the previous broker. If this isn't properly handled, it can be a "deal killer" later.

Another point to consider on the subject of listing agreements is the length of time that the agreement is valid. It's unreasonable to expect to sell a business in less than six months, with twelve months being a better estimate, given the complicated nature of the transaction. Consequently, a listing agreement should be for no less than six months, and realistically a year is a more reasonable term for both parties. If the seller is nervous about committing to one broker for that length of time, then insist on putting an escape clause in the agreement that lets the seller opt out after six months if the broker hasn't used reasonable best efforts (in the opinion of the seller) to sell the business.

To complete this chapter, the following are some interesting and important facts and figures concerning the purchase and sale of a small business.

Facts And Figures Regarding Buying Or Selling A Business

- There are approximately 5 million "real" businesses in the U.S. (if you include hobbiests, and sole practioners the number grows to 11 million) Of the "real" businesses; 80% have less than 10 employees and over 60% have 4 or less employees.

- At any given time there are about 1,000,000 (i.e. 20%) businesses on the market for sale; many of which will never be sold. The average selling price for a small business by a business broker is about $250,000.

- There are 4,000,000 potential business buyers for these companies but the vast majority will never buy a business. Most of these are not "qualified" buyers. (They lack either money, ability, desire/need, entrepreneurship or any combination).

- There are approximately 3,200 business brokerage firms, many hundreds of mergers and acquisition specialists, and hundreds more of investment banking companies.

- Even with the large number of businesses for sale, the huge pool of potential buyers, and the significant number of professional intermediaries, only about 20-25% of businesses for sale actually are sold their first time on the market.

- The bigger the business is (in sales volume and number of employees) the likelier it is to sell. Service businesses sell the most (42%) followed by food related (18%) and retail about 5%.

- For businesses with 1-4 employees only about 17% are actually sold. But, for businesses with 250+ employees the number that sell jumps to about 35% (the first time on the market).

- 1996 through 2001 has seen a dramatic increase in the number of strategically motivated buyers versus purely financial buyers.

- About 8% of all small businesses are franchises (and this number is growing).

- 80% of all small business sales involve the seller providing some form of financing for the buyer. Typically 50-75% of the purchase price.

- Business brokers report that 99% of the businesses they list for sale are not properly prepared to be sold. There can be many problems including:

    - Poor financial statements and/or disorganized legal ownership documentation

    - Outdated inventory and unprofitable products and/or services

    - Inefficient employee staffing

- Most potential business buyers don't buy because of:

    - Lack of understanding of the process which leads to uncertainty

    - Inability to raise enough funds (purchase money, professional fees, operating capital)

    - Fear of the unknown (the ability of the business to sustain past performance)

    - Fear that some key fact may have been misrepresented or omitted

Business Valuation

- *A Business Is An Investment*
- *Ways Of Purchasing A Business*
- *Hold Harmless Agreement*
- *Tangible And Intangible Assets*
- *Five Step Method To Valuing A Business*
- *Capitalization Of Available Cash Flow*
- *Other Ways Of Valuing A Business*
- *Examples Of Businesses With Typical ROI's*
- *Details Of Valuing The Business*
- *Unreported Cash Sales*
- *Financing The Purchase Of The Business*
- *Variables In The Business Valuation*
- *Comparing Business Operating Statistics*
- *Key Business Ratios*
- *Rules Of Thumb For Valuing A Business*

Now we come to one of the most important aspects of buying or selling a business – the price. One of the most pervasive and important laws of the business buying and selling jungle of all time prevails here; a business is worth only whatever someone is willing to pay for it at a particular point in time!

What this means is that there is no foolproof, absolutely accurate way of valuing anything, especially businesses. So how do buyers and sellers determine the value of a business so that they can begin negotiating with each other? I'll get to that shortly; but first, some background information. By the way, don't forget to use the glossary, Appendix H, if you run across any terms in this book that you're not familiar with and that I don't fully explain in the text. In the glossary, I've explained every key term used not only in this book, but other ones that you may run across in your efforts to buy or sell a business.

Strategic Jungle Law #3:

"A business is worth only whatever someone is willing to pay for it at a particular point in time!"

A Business Is An Investment

Don't forget, buyers and sellers are natural adversaries; the sellers want as much as they can get and the buyer wants to pay as little as possible. The broker is intensely interested too, because the commission amount is usually based on a percentage of the total selling price. However, both buyers and sellers should be aware that sometimes the broker's strongest objective may be to just close the deal at any price (a percentage of something is better than a percentage of nothing).

So, what process should you use to value a business? Forget about putting a value on the assets such as inventory, equipment, real estate, etc., based on resale value. Forget about comparing the business to the one in the next town or city that sold for a particular amount. Forget about all the "rules of thumb" like 8 times earnings or 5 times gross income or some dollar amount per account or any other shortcut formula that someone who doesn't know what they're doing can come up with. (My particular favorite of these useless ways of valuing businesses is the one I heard about hairdressing salons; $10,000 per hairdressing station). Apparently, that amount is independent of whether the business is profitable or not!

A business value, and therefore its selling price, only makes sense when it's based on the earnings stream, also known as the excess earnings or net profit. Both of these terms, the earnings stream and excess earnings can be thought of simply as the available cash flow. Capitalization is a complex word with a relatively straightforward meaning: the process used to determine today's value of a stream of future earnings. In our case of valuing a business, "today's value" is the value of the business, and the "stream of future earnings" is the expected available cash flow of the business based on current profits. Therefore, to keep things easy to follow, and to reduce unnecessary jargon in this book, I'll refer to this valuation concept as the Capitalization of Available Cash Flow. What this concept really means is that a business is an investment which is only as good as the money it provides for its owner(s).

Of course, there are other reasons to buy a business that could play into its selling price. For example, a burned-out Wall Street executive may be willing to buy a quaint, quiet, bed and breakfast in Vermont for a price that only breaks even, just to escape the rat race. Some laid-off workers may be willing to buy a business that only pays them a modest salary with no profit, just so they can have some control over their livelihood rather than go to work for another heartless employer. This is sometimes called "buying a job." For the most part, you can forget valuing a business based on these rare circumstances. Most businesses are sold strictly on the perceived bottom line. I say "perceived" because bottom lines can be kind of squishy.

In the rest of this chapter I'll take you through a detailed valuation of a business based on a capitalization of the available cash flow approach. This will give you sound fundamentals on which to determine the value of your business if you're a seller or to assess what you should pay for a business for sale if you're a buyer. Of course, this whole subject of business valuation can become quite complicated and can have some variations based on the kind of businesses involved. However, the capitalization of available cash flow approach presented in this book is based on sound economic principles that form the basis for valuing the vast majority of businesses for sale, large or small.

There are also other reasons for valuing a business that may have a direct bearing on the approach that's taken to valuation. For example, a business may be valued for:

- Litigation purposes
- Divorce settlements
- Resolution of disagreements between shareholders
- Estate and gift tax considerations
- Employee stock ownership plans (ESOP's)

For the purposes of this book, I'll focus on valuing a business to establish a fair market valuation to be used by buyers and sellers as they move to negotiations in an open and competitive marketplace. The actual sales price of a business will ultimately be the direct result of the give and take of negotiations between the buyer and seller, based on the fundamental laws of supply and demand.

Ways Of Purchasing A Business

There are some other important points that you need to understand. There are basically two ways to purchase an operating business for sale:

1. Purchase its assets (even if it's an incorporated business)

2. Purchase its corporate stock (only if it's an incorporated business)

I generally recommend against a buyer purchasing the corporate stock if a business is incorporated, except in the much more sophisticated situations involving many shareholders, subsidiary operations, complicated ownership of assets involving extensive liens and notes, etc. For the vast majority of operating business transactions, even if the business is currently operating as a legal corporation, conducting an asset purchase and sale is usually the best course of action. The business assets in this case are purchased from the corporation rather than from the unincorporated owner. Yes, you can still purchase a trade name, customer lists, employee contracts, copyrights, etc., that are not always thought of as assets that are easily transferred. I'll discuss this further later in this chapter.

The main reason that you don't want to purchase corporate stock is because of the potential unknown contingent liability that goes with it. A hidden creditor could suddenly arise, a past disgruntled employee with discrimination claims or compensation issues, an injured customer from several years ago that's late in bringing a claim against the company, unpaid state or federal income taxes, etc., etc. It's true that you may be able to get the corporate seller to give you a "hold harmless" agreement that pertains to any hidden liabilities that originated during the seller's ownership, but the corporation you purchased may still be liable and you may still have to spend significant amounts of time and money on legal fees to protect yourself, even if you didn't own the corporation at the time.

Ultimately though, the structure of the purchase and sale of a business is usually predominantly a legal and tax consequence issue. I strongly recommend that you receive good advice in these areas from your respective legal counsels and accountants. For most small to medium size business sales to an unrelated person, the asset-based sale is the best route, but corporate stock sales are done every day too, with little harm to the buyers if the transaction is structured properly.

Hold Harmless Agreement

I mentioned a "hold harmless" agreement in the previous section that you should certainly seek from the sellers of the shares (the shareholders) in a corporate stock sale. But, I also strongly recommend that any buyer of a business in any form (asset or stock sale) receive a "hold harmless" agreement from the seller. This agreement should be written to indemnify a buyer against any hidden, unknown, and/or unreported claims against any of the assets of the business resulting from the seller's prior operation of the business. Of course, this won't protect a buyer from their own actions after the sale, and it may not stop someone from filing a claim against the assets of the newly acquired business based on prior activity; but at least the buyer will have some protection of their investment.

The actual form of the "hold harmless" agreement will be highly specific to the type of business being purchased and to what the seller will actually agree to. The buyer should seek competent legal advice for this, and it's a good practice to let the seller know early in the negotiations for the business that you'll be asking for an agreement of this nature. I've included an example of a "Hold Harmless Agreement" as Appendix B so that you can see what one might look like.

Tangible And Intangible Assets

In an asset sale, you buy (or sell) only the assets of the business (with or without liens), and the corporation is left to the seller to legally dissolve or use in some other way unrelated to the business being sold. Either way, corporate stock or asset sale, you still need to identify the assets themselves to determine what makes up the business. There are basically two types of assets and some of the typical assets that you'll purchase include:

Tangible Assets	Intangible Assets
• Fixtures	• Trade Name, Trademarks
• Equipment	• Patents, Licenses, or Franchises
• Real Estate (land, buildings, leases)	• Seller's Covenant Not To Compete
• Inventory	• Customer Lists
• Accounts Receivable	• Customized Tooling and Dies
• Seller Service Contract	• Copyrights (including software)
• Employee Contracts	• Leasehold Interests
• Customer Contracts	• Proprietary Information
• Open Customer Orders	

Tangible assets are generally things that you can see, touch, feel, count, or measure, and for which you are generally able to provide an accepted fair market value. Such things as listed in the previous table include inventory, equipment, contracts, etc. Intangible assets are generally things that exist more in perception than in physical substance and have a specified life to them, and consequently are much more difficult to value. Using the valuation approach described in this book will make this process much simpler and straightforward.

Five Step Method To Valuing A Business

Before we get into the actual details of business valuation, first let me tell you about the major steps you need to follow to value a business for sale that has a profitable operating history, and then I'll tell you how to do each step. As I walk you through this, I'll use a real life example of an operating business to illustrate each point.

Step 1.   You need to obtain accurate (ideally, audited or certified) copies of the latest Income and Expense Statements for the business.

Step 2.   You need to analyze the Income and Expense Statements and reconstruct the income and expenses as appropriate (don't worry, I'll cover what this means).

Step 3.   After you have a Reconstructed Income and Expense Statement, you'll need to capitalize the available cash flow of the business according to a return on investment (ROI) which is appropriate for your expectations, and the risks involved in small business ownership, to arrive at a preliminary valuation.

Step 4.   After you have calculated the preliminary value, you'll need to add the value of the inventory and any other non-capitalized assets to determine the overall value of the business.

Step 5.   Finally, you'll need to tentatively distribute the overall business value between the various tangible and intangible assets. This apportionment of the value will most likely become part of the negotiations between the buyer and seller. This last step is also important because this is where you determine the actual business assets that you are going to purchase.

Capitalization Of Available Cash Flow

Okay, let's get to the detail of how to value (or evaluate the asking price) of a business using the capitalization of available cash flow approach. There's still some background discussion of important concepts we need to go through before we can get to applying the five-step valuation process outlined in the previous section, so please don't skip ahead.

Capitalization of Available Cash Flow is a powerful way of valuing a business which allows a business to be fairly evaluated as an investment opportunity without many of the uncertainties that other valuation methods introduce. This method assumes that business owners are entitled to a fair return on the value of the business (their investment) over and above their fair wage if the owners work in the business. The Small Business Administration (SBA) recommends a form of this approach to business valuation. The actual approach in this book is the author's own based on sound business practices and real life experiences in buying and selling businesses. This approach works equally well whether the business to be purchased is operating as a sole proprietorship or as a corporation!

One of the variables that we have to worry about when using this method is the "fair return" percentage. Because the ownership of a small business is a somewhat risky investment and future profits aren't guaranteed, a return on investment (ROI) of 20% to 25% isn't an unreasonable range of return to be expected. However, this range may even be too low in many service related businesses that have a low start-up cost, little or no inventory, and "soft" accounts; in other words, riskier businesses. In these types of riskier businesses, a 30% to 35% ROI is a good range of percentages to use. Conversely, a long established business with a solid reputation and stable or growing revenues may be more fairly valued using a 10-15% ROI.

Once a selling value is arrived at using the capitalization method, all of the assets are physically listed with an approximate value apportioned to them (except for the finished inventory, if any, which should be separately valued). This constitutes the appraised overall value of the business that's for sale. You should understand that the difference in price between the valuation using the capitalization of available cash flow method, and the fair market value of the tangible assets of the business, is assigned to the intangible assets of the business; usually called the goodwill. I know that this may not be totally clear at this point, but I'll demonstrate this concept later in the chapter. This procedure automatically accounts for the value of all tangible and intangible assets without actually considering them individually. The justification for this valuation method is another law of the business buying/selling jungle:

Strategic Jungle Law #4:

"A business buyer is really buying a stream of earnings!"

The assets of the business are just the tools of the trade that enable the earnings stream to be realized. Without the earnings stream, the business, as an investment, essentially has no value. You should note that in using this method, a business may actually be worth less than its fair market asset value or in many cases worth substantially more. A seller will be able to get the most they can for a business by showing a buyer the investment value in the business.

In many cases, buyers will pay the capitalization of available cash flow valuation of a business rather than its asset value (if the asset value is lower). It's much harder to get buyers to pay the asset value of a business if a reasonable return on investment isn't available.

Other Ways Of Valuing A Business

In the previous paragraph, I said "without the earnings stream, the business essentially has no value." This is fundamentally true when a buyer is purchasing an operating, profitable business that the buyer intends to continue to operate as an investment. However, I've already discussed other motivations for buyers in Chapter 1, and I'll also discuss this subject further in Chapter 3. At this point though, I want you to know that some businesses without earnings may have substantial value in the breaking up and selling of some parts of the asset base and therefore, this value may be based on things other than earnings. For example:

- Any business with an extensive, modern machine tool base or otherwise valuable equipment

- Any business with desirable real estate as part of the sale

- Any business with an assignable lease for a highly desirable business location (some businesses have been purchased only for the opportunity of obtaining the rights to a very favorable long-term lease for a commercial location). For example, I brokered the sale of a chain of women's shoe stores that sold for the principal reason that the buyer wanted the very valuable long-term leases (10 to 20 years) that went with the business. This was during a time of high inflation and dramatically escalating rents in the malls where these shoe stores were mainly located. The buyer eventually sub-let most of the business sites at a handsome profit and after a few years had no shoe stores left.

- Any business with valuable assignable rights, licenses, patents, copyrights, trademarks, etc. I once brokered the sale of a small manufacturing business that to my surprise was immediately shut down after the purchase. It turned out that the buyer really only wanted the rights to the patent for the product that was being manufactured. He soon after licensed the rights to another manufacturing company and apparently made out very well in the transaction.

These types of businesses generally are not offered on the market as "businesses for sale", but rather are offered as a specific sale of a particular asset.

Examples Of Businesses With Typical ROI's

The following businesses are a few examples of high asset value and relatively low return (lower capitalized value):

- Indoor Tennis Clubs/Country Clubs/Marinas
- Auto Dealerships/Hotels/Motels
- Restaurant/Inn Combinations
- Any business coupled with prime real estate or extensive valuable tangible assets

The following businesses are a few examples of low asset value and relatively high return (higher capitalized value):

- Advertising and Travel Agencies
- Opticians
- Professional Placement Agencies
- Distributorships
- Beauty Salons/Interior Decorators
- Any business with little or no real estate or very little tangible assets

Details Of Valuing
The Business

Now that we've covered the basic concepts, I'll take you through the details of the five-step business valuation process.

> ***Step 1:***   **Obtain accurate copies of the latest Income and Expense Statements and other related financial information for the business.**

This is a crucial part of valuing the business. You can't properly evaluate the business operation until you can examine its lifeblood; the operating income and expenses. The best and only two sources I recommend for this information is the business's Federal IRS Tax Return or an Audited Financial Statement from the latest full fiscal year, with the previous three years preferred. The reason I recommend three years worth of financial information is because to a buyer, a financial track record is extremely important in building confidence that profits can be expected to continue. If only one year's financial information is provided, the buyer won't know whether that year was out of the ordinary and therefore, won't know how to reasonably predict the future profitability of the business. Some business sellers may artificially improve the operating performance of their business in the year before a sale to enhance its value. Of course, some efforts by the seller to improve performance of the business are fully legitimate and actually represent a clearer picture of the real operating characteristics of the business. I'll discuss this topic further in Chapter 5 in the section "Preparing A Business For Sale." The best situation is if the financial records show an increasing profit picture for at least two additional reasons:

1. The seller may be able to justify a higher price for the business based on the projected next year's higher profits rather than the current year's.

2. The buyer will realize that the seller has other options than selling to him. The seller can keep the business and continue to pocket the profits or find a more amenable buyer. These facts should work in the seller's favor in demanding a higher price for the business.

If you're the business seller and you're doing your own business valuation, this is easy; either you have them or you can get them from your accountant. However, if you're the buyer, you'll probably encounter some difficulty. The seller will naturally be very reluctant to provide access to these documents to just anyone as they contain very private and confidential information. My recommendation is that a seller should provide the latest three years of IRS Tax Returns or Audited Financial Statements to a buyer for their evaluation, but only after two important steps have been taken:

- A Confidentiality Agreement has been signed by the buyer
- A Buyers Financial Qualifications Statement has been submitted

A Confidentiality Agreement is a very important document that's signed by the buyer and delivered to the seller. This Agreement is intended to protect from unauthorized disclosure, the sensitive and private information that is provided by the seller to the buyer during negotiations. This Confidentiality Agreement can be entered into before or after the Earnest Money Agreement are signed, but always before sensitive, private, and specific financial information about the business is provided to the potential buyer, such as IRS Income Tax Returns or audited financial statements. I've included an example of a Confidentiality Agreement as Appendix D. Most good professional business brokers, as part of their process in qualifying a potential buyer, will have the buyer execute a Confidentiality Agreement before any significant sensitive information concerning the business for sale is disclosed.

The Buyers Financial Qualifications Statement has been previously discussed in Chapter 1 and an example is provided as Appendix E.

There are other financial based documents that you should also carefully consider when evaluating the business. Using the capitalization of available cash flow approach lessens the analysis that you need to apply to this other information to arrive at a business valuation. However, you should certainly accomplish due diligence in satisfying yourself that the information presented to you is true and current, and assess any impact that this information could have on the value of the business. Due diligence is a commonly accepted term in the business purchase and sale field that refers to a process of investigation by the buyer into a business's operating and financial performance and a rigorous verification of material facts affecting the business for sale. Most of this other financial information can be analyzed after an Earnest Money Agreement has been entered into and can be evaluated on a contingency basis based on satisfactory verification of the presented information. Some of the documentation you should ask for and review as part of your due diligence are:

- Balance Sheet (list of assets, liabilities, and net worth)
- Accounts Receivable (I recommend that you don't purchase this asset of the company because sometimes the accounts aren't fully collectible)

- Inventory Listing (work in process and finished goods)

- Real Estate (a separate real estate appraisal based on present use rather than highest and best use should be used)

- Machinery and Equipment Lists (an independent appraisal of fair market value should be used)

- Accounts Payable (try to ensure that all accounts are current and that you don't buy any debt)

- Accrued Liabilities (you may have to assume these as part of the business and the business valuation should be adjusted downward accordingly)

- Promissory Notes and Mortgages (buyers shouldn't assume as part of the business purchase any notes and mortgages payable unless the terms are more favorable than they can otherwise get)

- Leases (carefully review the terms and conditions to determine future impacts on the business)

- Proof of the seller's ownership and rights to assets

- "Key employee" contracts

- Significant sales contracts, warranties, and related documentation binding upon the business for sale

I've provided a much more detailed look at the due diligence process in Chapter 4.

Step 2: **Analyze and reconstruct the Income and Expense Statements**

This step is critical to properly value the operating business for sale and will require some investigation and business intuition on your part. Both the buyer and seller should carefully accomplish this step for the same reasons; identifying the real value in the business. I've sprung a new phrase on you here that refers to the "real value" in a business. This is as opposed to the "hidden value." The reason we need to deal with this issue is because many businesses are operated in such a way as to maximize the direct benefit to the owner and to minimize the tax exposure to the IRS. Most of the ways this is done are fully legitimate, and some fall into a gray area. We need to identify these "hidden value" areas and add them back to the overall operation of the business to give us a clearer picture of the actual benefits (money) that a new business owner can expect to realize from the business. Of course, the seller and the buyer will want to make the numbers come out in their respective favor so there will necessarily be some give and take in this area during negotiations. But for now, let's just go through the process and understand the fundamentals.

Let's discuss what I mean when I use the term business expense reconstruction. This reconstruction will assist you in identifying the hidden values and/or hidden costs in a business operation. I'll give you an example of what I mean. Let's say the XYZ Company pays all the expenses for a company car which is used principally for the private benefit of the business owner (never mind that the IRS would take a dim view of this if they knew; that part is the seller's problem, not the buyer's). When you value the company, that car should not be an expensed item because it's not really needed in the running of the business. The expenses for that car should be deleted in the reconstruction of the expenses, which will decrease the overall expenses, thus increasing the income, and therefore increase the valuation of the business. After you purchase the business, you can choose not to continue this expense item and will instead have the cash available for your other use.

Another example of a reconstructed expense is the owner's salary or draw from the business which isn't sufficient to cover the time and effort involved at a fair market wage. Let's say that the business owner is also the full-time manager of the business, and the salary is $40,000 per year. The fair market wage to hire a manager for that position is $60,000. In this case the reconstructed expense should be increased by $20,000 to account for the underpayment of the business owner. This will increase the overall expenses, thus decreasing the income, and therefore decrease the valuation of the business. Sometimes you'll find that business owners are overpaying themselves or others in the business, and you'll want to subtract out the difference between the actual wages paid and the fair market value of that wage. Of course, this will have the opposite effect on the ultimate valuation of the business. I know that this might be a little confusing, but it's important to understand. We'll soon go over a real life example that will make it all much clearer. The following are some common add/subtract expense items which you should consider when you're reconstructing an income and expense sheet:

Examples of Income Reconstruction Items

Add:

+ Operating income earned but not credited to the current year (e.g. the business may be on a cash accounting basis rather than accrual accounting with significant income earned for the current fiscal year but not yet received).

Subtract:

- Interest earned on cash deposits in banks or other institutions.

- Interest earned on loans or other items.

- Extraordinary income not related to continuing business operations (e.g. capital gains on business investments, sale of surplus equipment, etc.).

Examples Of Expense Reconstruction Items

Add:

+ Owner's wage below currently prevailing fair market wage

+ Planned increase in rent or any other increasing recurring costs

+ Increase in advertising and/or marketing costs to revitalize a sagging business

+ Increase in expenses to replace aging equipment

+ Any other planned expense increases

Subtract:

- Owner's wage over the currently prevailing fair market wage

- Excess depreciation over what is actually needed to cover replacement costs (the IRS lets businesses deduct this but many times it's not an actual expense)

- Excess amortization over the actual value decline of the asset

- Interest payments for debt that the buyer will not assume (the business debt costs will most likely be different and will be covered later under the valuation process)

- Excess advertising over what is actually needed

- Excess auto usage (personal use)

- Excess travel and entertainment (personal use)

- Salaries to be eliminated (unnecessary employees)

- Non-recurring expenses and those that should have been capitalized

- All other excessive expenses

- Donations that you don't plan to continue

- Key person life insurance provided for the benefit of the owner

As one last example of a potential reconstructed expense item that isn't black and white, I'll tell you about my experience with "Fifi, the junkyard dog." I had listed a large automobile junkyard for sale that sold the recovered parts of vehicles for sale through several retail outlets, as well as selling the scrap metal. Business was very good, and sales exceeded $1,000,000. As I worked with the seller to reconstruct the expenses to find "hidden value", I noticed an expenditure for costs related to a "junkyard dog." The expenses were relatively large covering veterinarian bills, dog food, and periodic kenneling. I had been in the junkyard with the seller when it was closed, and I had never seen a dog. When I questioned the seller about this, he said "Oh, that's Fifi, my wife's toy poodle. Once in a while we bring the dog out here, but she's really a house pet." So here's an obvious benefit to the seller that's not an actual business expense. The junkyard didn't really need "Fifi, the junkyard dog" because there was a modern electronic security system already in place that apparently worked fine. The expenses related to Fifi could perhaps be added back in the expense reconstruction, but as I said at the start of this anecdote, it's not black and white. First, the IRS would probably not appreciate the junkyard owner's handling of this as an expense item for the business. Second, it's hard to verify that this actually was an expense for Fifi and not some other legitimate expense for a real guard dog on the chance that the electronic security system doesn't really work well. I'll leave it up to the reader as to how they want to deal with these gray areas. However, sellers should take note that many buyers will be getting into details such as this as they consider buying the business. Sellers should begin preparing their businesses for sale at least a year in advance of offering it on the market by "cleaning up" their income and expenses. I'll talk more about this in Chapter 5.

For the rest of this discussion, it's easier to understand if we deal with a real life business situation to illustrate the points. For our purposes, let's consider the XYZ Company which is a privately-held company that has been in business for about 25 years. The owner wants to retire and has made a very nice living from the company and doesn't mind selling the business under a financing arrangement to a qualified buyer. We don't need to concern ourselves with the type of business that the XYZ Company is for valuation purposes; we only need to understand how much net profit will be available to a buyer as a result of business operations. Here are some pertinent points we need to know before we take a hard look at the expense sheet:

- The company has had stable or moderately (1% to 5%) increasing sales and profit for each of its 25 years, and its projected gross revenues for the next full financial year are $350,000.

- All current and long-term liabilities of the company will be dissolved by the owner at the time of sale (accounts payable, notes and mortgages payable, liens, etc.).

- There are no accrued liabilities for a buyer to concern themselves with (unpaid wages, unpaid employee benefits, taxes, etc.).

- A recent "present use" appraisal of the real estate to be conveyed as part of the business sale came in at $250,000.

- The depreciated current value of the furnishings and equipment is $150,000 which happens to correspond to the fair market value if these items were sold independently.

- The estimated value of the inventory including work in process and finished goods is $50,000 (the actual value will be adjusted up or down at the closing).

- The company has a well-known trade name in its field and its principal product has a registered trademarked name. Both the trade name and the trademark will be transferred as part of the business purchase and sale.

- The principal product is produced under a wholly-owned patent that has ten years remaining to its life. This patent is to be transferred to the buyer as part of the purchase and sale of the business.

- The sale of the business will be an asset sale even though it's currently operating as a corporation. After the sale of the business the seller will take the necessary steps to dissolve the corporation by filing the proper forms with the Secretary of State in the state in which it's incorporated.

Now that we have these necessary facts about the XYZ Company that are obtained by reviewing the business's financial statements, including the balance sheet and other information gathered about the business as part of the buyer's due diligence, it's time to take a look at the Income and Expense Statement for the purposes of reconstruction. First, we'll look at the expenses that are described in the following table of data. I'll then talk about reconstructing the income.

Example: XYZ Company Expense Reconstruction

Item	Statement Expense	Reconstructed Expense	Reason For Difference
Leased Equipment	12,000	13,200	Lease requirement increases payment from $1,000/month to $1,100/ month in the next year
Owner's Wage	60,000	45,000	$15,000 of wages excessive for a comparable employee
Employee Salaries	100,000	66,000	$34,000 for owner's brother-in-law not needed
Client Entertain.	4,000	2,000	$2,000 owner's personal benefit (trip to Las Vegas)
Interest	5,000	0	Not required business expense. Business debt will not be assumed by the buyer, but will be paid off by the seller at transfer
Auto	6,000	0	Owner's personal benefit (car not needed in business operations)
Repair & Maint.	10,000	8,000	$2,000 non-recurring cost in last year
Depreciation	20,000	10,000	Accelerated depreciation of amount actually necessary to hold in reserve for equipment replacement ($10,000 excess depreciation)
Amortization	5,000	0	Not a cash outlay. Portion of price paid for patent to be transferred with the business
All Other Expenses	44,000	44,000	No adjustment. Expenses are expected to continue
Total Expenses	$266,000	$188,200	

I've been talking about reconstructing the Income and Expense Statement, and all I've talked about so far is expenses. For the most part, there is little or no reconstruction to be done on the income side of the ledger. If a business owner has been reporting income from sales of a certain amount on the IRS Tax Returns for several years, and is therefore paying federal, state, and local taxes on that income, it's reasonable to assume that in fact, the business has had that income.

However, there are at least two reasons to consider reconstructing the income as well:

- Unreported cash sales

- Extraordinary income that is recorded in the wrong year (e.g., a large account pays its December bill in January of the next year — the income may be rightfully adjusted into the previous year to reflect true business activity)

Unreported Cash Sales

Now let's talk about a very sensitive subject known as unreported (to the IRS) cash sales. Some business sellers may try to get you to accept their claim that they had significant amounts of cash income that didn't show up on their IRS Tax Return and accordingly want you to include this income in your valuation of their business. I highly recommend that you totally ignore these claims and deal only with the business's reported income for the following reasons:

- Unreported cash sales constitute tax fraud, and you don't want to make yourself party to the possible fraudulent actions of others.

- Unreported cash sales are difficult, if not impossible, to validate.

- You'll never get any reputable financial institution to loan purchase funds to you on the basis of unsubstantiated income.

- If the seller cheats the IRS on the business's income taxes, how can you be sure that you're being dealt with honestly in regard to the entire collection of information about the business?

I feel so strongly about this point that I've made it a law of the jungle:

Strategic Jungle Law #5:

"Ignore all claims of unreported income!"

There are some businesses known in the business brokerage trade that have a certain notoriety for unreported cash sales; but that doesn't necessarily mean that any particular one is guilty of this. In fact, the vast majority of quality businesses would never jeopardize their business reputation (not to mention taking the risk of criminal prosecution!). Typically any business with large amounts of cash revenues is a potential for unreported cash sales. Some of the businesses that have been known to have a fair amount of unreported cash sales include:

- Vending routes
- Restaurants
- Amusement arcades
- Beauty parlors
- Convenience stores
- Automotive junk yards

I know of one potential buyer of a restaurant who tried to validate unreported cash sales by picking a two-week period at random from the financial records from the previous year and working side-by-side with the seller during the comparable two-week period in the current year to see if there was any truth to the restaurant owner's claim. My understanding is that this undertaking gave more validation to another rather harsh law of the jungle that:

Strategic Jungle Law #6:

*"Most sellers are liars!
(or they at least stretch the truth)"*

Of course, this is not really a completely true law of the jungle. Most sellers are honest people trying to get by in life like everyone else. However, a buyer should approach all information provided in the sale with some skepticism. Buyers are making a major financial decision and should carefully consider all information presented. If a seller tries to claim that they have large amounts of unreported cash sales, that means the seller may be cheating the government. Does this give a buyer a good feeling that the seller won't cheat them, too? If a buyer approaches the purchase of a business with a good healthy dose of "prove it to me," then it will be difficult for them to get burned.

Step 3: **Capitalize the available cash flow from the reconstructed Income and Expense Statement**

Now that we have reconstructed the Income and Expense Statement and have estimated the amount of gross available cash flow, we'll need to convert it to net available cash flow by accounting for income taxes. Then we need to "capitalize" the available cash flow (convert future earnings into a present value) using a selected return on investment (ROI). This may sound complicated, but in reality the math is easy. The hard part is determining the income tax rate and the ROI to use. Earlier in this chapter I addressed the ranges of ROI's for different types of businesses, and I'll summarize them here:

- Long established business with excellent earnings records and substantial tangible assets necessary to the business operation — 15% to 20% ROI's are reasonable

- Established businesses with good earnings records and some tangible assets — 20% to 25% ROI's are reasonable

- Riskier businesses with so-so earnings records and very little tangible assets — 25% to 35% ROI's are reasonable

The actual choice of what ROI to use is a personal one and subject to the buyer's and seller's interpretations of business stability, earnings history, future growth prospects, etc. There's no magic formula, and every situation is different. I strongly recommend that the buyer carefully consider all risk factors involved, and make the best choice for themselves. In general, the broad ranges I've offered here should work equally well for both the buyer and the seller.

The most important aspect of the ROI selection is that it should be based on future expectations of net profits for the business being considered. In our example of the XYZ Company, we know that the business is long-established, with stable moderate sale and profit growth (1% to 5% per year). We can reasonably expect sales and profits for the next few years to continue at the current levels with small to moderate increases needed to account for any inflation concerns. Accordingly, for valuation purposes we'll use a ROI in the low end of the range: 20%.

One additional very important point that the buyer and seller should keep in mind: the ROI selected should never be less than the cost of the money (the interest rate charged) that needs to be borrowed to finance the business purchase. For example, if the lowest bank financing available is at 12%, then that should establish the absolute minimum ROI that a buyer will use in computing the capitalized value of the business. However, the buyer needs to cover not only the financing costs necessary to purchase the business, but should also look for a fair return on the total cash invested in the business. Also, even the best of businesses are risky, and therefore a buyer should look for a higher than normal return as compared to alternative investments to justify the overall risk that they're taking.

Sellers and buyers should keep in mind that if the seller is going to hold some or all of the financing of the business purchase, the value of the business can be affected (up and down) by the interest rate negotiated. This will be covered much more extensively in the section in Chapter 6 on "Conducting Negotiations."

Now that you have a good idea about which ROI you want to use, you have to select an income tax rate to convert gross income to net income for capitalization purposes. After all, you've got to pay Uncle Sam and in many cases, municipal and state taxes too. Income taxes are a necessary evil of profitable businesses. The income tax rate, like the ROI, is a very personal number in that the graduated rate nature of our federal income tax structure and the dramatically varied rates from state to state are related directly to the way each of us chose to operate our businesses (sole proprietorship, partnership, corporation, subchapter-S corporation, limited liability company, etc.). You must select the tax rate that you, the buyer, expect to have to pay. As the seller, use your current rate and leave any differences between the buyer's and seller's rate to the negotiation process. For the purposes of this book, I'll use a fairly representative average rate of 40%. Buyers, be sure to consult with a professional accountant so that you have a good idea of what income tax rate you should use.

Okay, let's get to the math part of this now that you've tentatively picked a ROI and an income tax rate with which you're comfortable.

Here's what we want to calculate:

Capitalized Value = Available Cash Flow divided by ROI (as a decimal)

(Note: use our XYZ Company example to work out these numbers)

First: Calculate Gross Available Cash Flow (ACF)

Gross ACF	= Gross Revenue minus Reconstructed Total Expenses
	= \$350,000 – \$188,200
	= \$161,800

Second: Calculate Net Available Cash Flow (ACF)

Net ACF	= Gross ACF multiplied by (1.0 minus the Income Tax Rate {as a decimal}). Note: 40% = .40 as a decimal.
	= \$161,800 x (1.0 – .40)
	= \$161,800 x (.60)
	= \$97,080

Third: Calculate Capitalized Value

Capitalized Value = Net ACF divided by ROI (as a decimal)

Capitalized Value = \$97,080 / (.20) = \$485,400

See, I told you the math was easy!

Step 4:   **Determine the overall value of the business by adding in any non-capitalized assets**

First, let's define what I mean by non-capitalized assets. These are assets (also known as current assets) that are to be conveyed as part of the business purchase and are essentially the same as cash, i.e., they are easily converted to cash. Some examples are:

- Cash on hand (the buyer may be taking over the business checking account)

- Finished inventory (ready to be sold)

- Accounts receivable (money owed to the business)

The buyer must be very careful when buying finished inventory to make sure that it's in good condition, readily salable, no outdated products, etc. I've seen many post-sale disputes arise out of an argument about the actual value of inventory. I recommend that buyers carefully evaluate the finished inventory as close to the time of business sale closing as possible to verify its value and quantity. In fact, buyers may want to have an independent appraisal done of the business inventory.

During this valuation process and also during negotiations, it's usual to use a rough approximation of the inventory value. This is okay because the actual selling price of the business will be adjusted up or down at the closing based on a detailed determination of the inventory value at that time. This holds true for any other assets such as checking accounts and accounts receivable that are to be purchased and will vary during the normal course of business operations that are ongoing during the business purchase process.

I strongly recommend that buyers don't include the accounts receivable as part of the purchase of the business. Some unscrupulous creditors upon learning that the business has been sold may not honor their debt to the business, and some accounts may already be uncollectible. In almost all cases, the seller should take responsibility for collecting the accounts receivable themselves to avoid any post-sale problems with the buyer.

Again, using our example for the XYZ Company, assume that the seller will retain all of the cash on hand in the business and also that the seller will collect all accounts receivable. In this case the inventory is tentatively valued at $50,000 (both the seller and buyer have agreed to this value). We can now determine the overall business value by adding together the capitalized value and the inventory value:

> ### *Overall Business Value =*
>
> ### *Capitalized Value plus Non-Capitalized Asset Value*
>
> = Capitalized Value + Inventory Value (for XYZ Company)
>
> = $485,400 + $50,000
>
> = $535,400

We now know that the overall business value based on our assumptions is $535,400!

I want to insert a note of caution to both buyers and sellers at this point. Frequently, the original computed overall business value is substantially different between the buyer's and seller's calculations because of their different views of the numerous variables. Additionally, the actual selling price of the business may itself be substantially different than either the buyer's or seller's original calculations. The final selling price of the business will be based on the negotiations that take place between the buyer and seller and as more detailed information about the business and the terms and conditions of the structure of the sale are agreed upon. Later in this chapter, I'll highlight some of the variables that may change and in Chapter 6, "Conducting Negotiations," I'll talk more about their impact on the purchase and sale of the business.

Step 5: Distribute the overall business valuation between the various assets

Whew! We're almost there in having a business valuation from which buyers and sellers can begin negotiations. We have an overall business value based on a capitalization of available cash flow and next need to structure that value among the tangible and intangible assets for the purposes of negotiations, and for structuring the asset sale of the business. In the example just used, we arrived at a business value of $535,400. We've already determined the fair market value estimates for the tangible assets and real estate that are needed to be purchased to operate the business from earlier in this chapter:

Tangible Assets	Fair Market Value Estimate
Furnishings and equipment *(from balance sheet)*	$150,000
Real estate *(recent appraisal)*	$250,000
	$400,000

The difference between the overall business value of $535,400 and the tangible asset fair market value of $400,000 is $135,400. Now subtract out the non-capitalized assets (in our XYZ Company case, this is the inventory of $50,000 only) which results in a value of $85,400. This value is collectively referred to as the goodwill of the business and is assigned as a value to the intangible assets that are necessary to be purchased. For example:

Intangible Assets (Goodwill)	Assigned Value Estimate
Trade Name and Trademark	$10,000
Covenant Not To Compete	$50,000
Customer Lists	$ 5,000
Patents	$20,400
Total Goodwill	**$85,400**

The above allocation of values has been done somewhat arbitrarily for illustration purposes only for the XYZ Company example. The actual strategy of how to allocate the values to the intangible assets will be a matter of negotiation, but I'll offer some ideas here for both buyers and sellers to consider. I'll discuss this further in Chapter 6. For now, accept the fact that in general the buyer wants to minimize the amounts allocated to depreciable/amortizable assets as much as possible, because the amounts can only be deducted against income usually over many years. The seller generally wants to minimize funds to themselves that are paid as personal income. The seller generally prefers capital gain income (the tax rate is somewhat less) over personal income. But as of this writing, the difference between capital gains tax rates and personal income tax rates is so small that this shouldn't be a stumbling block between the buyer and seller. Some of the considerations that are negotiated between the buyer and seller relative to allocating the business purchase and sale price to various assets include:

• The trade name and trademarks are generally not depreciable assets or if they're depreciated, it's over a long period of time.

• The covenant not to compete may be amortized over its relatively short life by the buyer and expensed against the business's income.

• The customer lists are generally not a depreciable asset, so very little value (if any) is applied to them.

• The patents are depreciable assets over the life of the patent (usually a patent has an original life of 17 years; in our case 10 years of life are remaining).

This covers the general concepts of the five basic steps to determining the value for a profitable operating business, but we need to go one step further to see how the buyer can pay for the business.

Financing The Purchase Of The Business

What we've discussed so far in our valuation of the XYZ Company is:

- The business has $97,080 of excess net profit after all the expenses are covered (including a fair owner's wage and an allowance for income taxes).

- The business has a capitalized value of $485,400 plus $50,000 of current salable inventory for an overall valuation of $535,400.

Assuming the buyer is to offer this price to the seller who then accepts, how is the buyer going to pay for the business? First, assume that the buyer has $125,000 to invest in the business. Let's allocate the funds as follows:

	Allocation of Buyer's Cash	
	$ 25,000	For working capital (checking account, current payables, closing costs, etc.)
plus:	$100,000	Cash down payment to the seller
	$125,000	Total buyer's cash investment

The purchase situation now looks like this:

	Amount To Be Financed	
	$535,000	Total business purchase price
less:	$100,000	Cash down payment to the seller
	$435,400	Amount to be financed

We've already determined that the seller is willing to take a Promissory Note for some reasonable amount to finance the sale of the business. In reality, buyers could secure their own financing from their own resources; a bank, the SBA (also a bank loan but secured by the SBA), other types of lending institutions, venture capitalists, etc. Whatever the source of funds if the money is borrowed, the following calculations hold. Let's assume that the buyer offers, and the seller accepts, a ten-year promissory note for the entire balance of $435,400 at 12% compound interest. The payments will be:

$6,247/month which equals $74,964 per year

The available excess net profit which is actually the business's available cash flow after all operating expenses and income taxes is $97,080. This provides substantial funds to pay the promissory note. In fact:

Remaining Cash Flow

$97,080	Excess net profit
$74,964	Annual payments to seller
$22,116	Return on buyer's cash

$22,116 ÷ $125,000 x 100% = 17.7%

The percentage return on the buyer's cash
of $125,000 is almost 18%.

In this example of the XYZ Company, the buyer now owns the company for $125,000 out of pocket cash and total annual payments to the seller of $74,964 for ten years. The buyer will be receiving a fair wage for their efforts in the business as the promissory note is paid down, and will be realizing a return on the cash investment of nearly 18% per annum which is $22,116 of available free cash to reinvest in the business to grow the business base over time to further increase its value and profitability. At the end of ten years, the business will be fully paid off and the buyer can look forward to not only the fair market salary that will be available, but can also begin to take for personal or business expansion use, the $74,964 per year that was being paid to the seller. The seller, on the other hand, has received $100,000 cash, will be receiving $74,964 per annum for ten years, during which time the seller retains a mortgage interest in the business in the event the buyer doesn't fulfill the agreed upon obligations. The seller will have realized $100,000 plus 120 payments of $6,247 per month for a total income of $849,640 over ten years.

Of course, this is just an example and many complexities have been left out for clarity; but the fundamentals will remain the same for any business sale. If the numbers don't work out, then there are many variables that can be adjusted to make the deal work as long as there's a motivated buyer and seller and a profitable operating business.

Some of the details that will have to be worked out in an actual business sale which will directly affect the business selling price and the cash required from a buyer include:

- Is there enough cash coming out of the business sale for the seller to pay off the liens, mortgages, and other business debts that the buyer isn't assuming?

- Is there enough cash coming out of the business sale for the seller to pay the business broker's commission?

- How will the fees for the various professional advisors be covered (lawyers, accountants, appraisers, etc.)?

- How will the fees for the various municipal filings, licenses, permits, etc. be paid?

- What is the income tax exposure of the seller, and is there enough cash and income from the Promissory Note to cover these expenses?

Variables In The Business Valuation

Now let's discuss some of the variables that can be adjusted in the business valuation to affect the overall total valuation of the business. All of these variables would have a ripple effect on the XYZ Company example that we used, and many of the calculated numbers would change:

- The selected return on investment rate (ROI) could be changed.

- The selected expected income tax rate could be changed (and in some valuation approaches it is not used at all due to its situation-specific variability).

- The interest rate acceptable to the buyer as a return on the cash could be changed.

- The interest rate charged on the Promissory Note (whether seller financed or not) could be changed.

- The Promissory Note could be amortized over a longer or shorter period of time.

- The buyer could put more or less cash into the business purchase.

- The reconstruction of the Income and Expense Statement could be done differently (maybe the business really does need the services of the seller's brother-in-law).

- The seller could take part of the purchase price as a consulting contract over a period of time, which might lessen the need for up front cash from the buyer. This could lower the overall cost of the business, while still providing income to the seller.

Comparing Business Operating Statistics

Another good way to help evaluate the business that is being sold is to compare how it stacks up to other similar operating businesses. You usually can find compiled data for almost any kind of business that relates vital statistics about the business to such important operating data as sales, profits, number of employees, industry trends, number of businesses in your geographic area, etc. This data may give you a better feel about the business you're evaluating and may influence your selection of a ROI that the business will support. Both buyers and sellers should seek out this information (the library and Internet are good places to look) to use as part of the overall evaluation of the business opportunity, especially in helping you to determine positive or negative trends. The following are a few sources of this kind of business related data that I've used:

Dun & Bradstreet, Inc.
One Diamond Hill Road
Murray Hill, NJ 07974
http://www.DNB.com

Almanac of Business and Industrial Financial Ratios
Prentice-Hall, Inc.
Upper Saddle River, NJ 07458
http://www.PrenticeHall.com

Worldata, Inc.
5200 Town Center Circle
Boca Raton, FL 33486
http://www.Worldata.com

iMarket, Inc.
http://www.iMarketInc.com

For example, the Almanac of Business and Industrial Financial Ratios will provide you with the types of information listed below for businesses with particular Standard Industrial Classification (SIC) codes. You can use this information to see how the business under consideration for sale compares to other businesses of a similar nature. Some are:

- Number of businesses in United States grouped by asset size
- Average business revenues
- Average costs of operations (costs of goods/services sold)
- Average maintenance, repair, and rent costs
- Average taxes, depreciation, and advertising costs
- Net profits before tax
- Current and quick ratios
- Liability to net worth ratio
- Return on assets
- Net income to net worth ratio

As another example of data that you may want to examine, iMarket Inc. provides detailed information about thousands of different business types, also related to SIC codes, but from a different perspective. They compare businesses in a particular type:

- Overall market size is presented with information broken down on a national and state-by-state basis: numbers of employees, sales, market share, and company size.
- A further breakdown of information by business specialty types within the otherwise broad SIC codes. To give you an idea of the level they go to, I saw in one "Market Analysis by Specialty" section information on horse drawn carriage businesses of which there are 96 in the United States!

Key Business Ratios

As an end to this important chapter on Business Valuation, I'll provide you with some key business ratios that you may want to use in your evaluation of the business for sale. The Almanac of Business and Industrial Ratios, which I mentioned previously, is a good source for industry standards for these ratios.

Is the business solvent?

$$\frac{\text{Current Assets}}{\text{Current Liabilities}}$$

A test for solvency. Provides clues to the magnitude of the financial margin of safety. For more stringent tests, delete inventory from the assets and compute a new ratio.

Has the business borrowed wisely?

$$\frac{\text{Total Debt}}{\text{Net Worth}}$$

Reveals the extent to which the business has borrowed. Too much debt may indicate insufficient capital and could weaken the competitive position.

How is the business performing?

$$\frac{\text{Working Capital}}{\text{Sales}}$$

Shows relationships of working capital to business transactions. Compare with industry and related business averages to determine business performance.

Are the products selling?

$$\frac{\text{Costs of Sales}}{\text{Inventory}}$$

Shows number of times inventory turns over. Comparison with industry and related business averages can be revealing.

How's management doing?

$$\frac{\text{Net Profit}}{\text{Net Worth}}$$

Shows return on invested capital. Compare with industry and related business averages.

Is the business earning a profit?

$$\frac{\text{Net Profit}}{\text{Sales}}$$

This measures profit margins. Compare with industry and related business averages.

Are profits adequate?

$$\frac{\text{Cost of Sales}}{\text{Sales}}$$

If this margin appears thin compared to industry average, it could mean trouble. This indicates how much money is available to pay expenses.

As I previously mentioned, the Dun & Bradstreet, Inc. company is also a great source of key business ratios that you can use to compare the financial operations of the business being considered for purchase and sale with other businesses in the same industry category. Business ratio data that they collect and which you may obtain from them includes:

- Current assets to current debt
- Net profits on net sales
- Net profits on tangible net worth
- Net profits on net working capital
- Net sales to tangible net worth
- Net sales to net working capital
- Collection period
- Net sales to inventory
- Fixed assets to tangible net worth
- Current debt to tangible net worth
- Total debt to tangible net worth
- Inventory to net working capital
- Current debt to inventory
- Funded debts to net working capital

Rules Of Thumb For Valuing A Business

I've been asked many times about the use of "rules of thumb" for determining the value of a business. While I don't recommend this approach for actually determining the selling price of a business, knowing the rules of thumb used by business brokers can have substantial value. Rules of thumb can give you a quick idea about the ballpark value of a business without the extensive (and expensive) process of a full-blown appraisal. If you're early in the decision process about buying or selling a particular business and you want to determine an approximate selling price, then using generally accepted rules of thumb determined by business brokers based on actual transactions may be very helpful to you.

For example:*

- Gas stations sell for 2.5 – 3.0 times available cash flow

- Restaurants sell for 2.0 – 4.0 times available cash flow (depending on the type)

- Gift Shops sell for about 30% of annual sales plus inventory

- Motels sell for 2.5 – 3.0 times room revenues or $20,000 per room

- Medical Practices sell for 20 – 60% of fee revenues with an earnout requirement

- Manufacturing companies sell for 1.5 – 4.0 times available cash flow

The absolute best published source for these rules of thumb I've found are in The Business Reference Guide (updated annually). It contains over 500 different rules of thumb for over a hundred different types of businesses and includes a tremendous amount of detail about the buying, selling and valuing of a business. Although this is primarily a resource for business brokers, it contains much valuable insider information that many buyers and sellers of businesses will find extremely valuable. You can find this extensive 700+ page guide online at www.BusinessBookPress.com or use the order form provided in the back of this book.

---

* Reprinted with permission from Tom West, editor, *The Business Reference Guide*, 11th edition. The actual rules of thumb for the above listed business contain much more information for each type of business. For example, Restaurants are broken down into dozens of different categories with various types of rules of thumb and even classified by different parts of the country.

3

Buyers Seeking Sellers

- *Examine Your Motivations To Buy A Business*
- *Sources Of Information On Businesses For Sale*
- *Motivation For Sellers To Sell*
- *Buying An Existing Franchise*
- *Turnaround Situations*
- *Business Location*
- *Number Of Businesses For Sale*
- *Key Questions To Ask A Business Seller*
- *Checklist Of Steps For Buying A Business*

Before I get too far into giving you information about how to find high quality, profitable, operating businesses for sale, I want to do at least part of what I do with all new potential buyers that come to me. I obviously can't determine your financial qualifications, but I want you to evaluate yourself relative to your ability to run a business.

Examine Your Motivations To Buy A Business

I want you to verify that you're really a motivated buyer. This isn't done just to save the broker and seller time by weeding out the non-buyers, but also to save the buyers from themselves. Sometimes potential buyers who have no business buying a business will find themselves the new owner of an ongoing business and then disaster strikes; they suffer financial loss, their mental and physical health deteriorates, they lose their relationship with their families etc. This can occur because they weren't qualified or able to deal with the challenges of running a business.

Here's a checklist of considerations that may apply to you and the situation you are, or will be, evaluating. Carefully go through this list, and consider your own ability to handle each item before you commit yourself to owning a small business.

- ❏ Do you know what kind of business you want to buy?

- ❏ Are you "technically" qualified and experienced enough to run the business?

- ❏ Do you have the temperament to deal with fickle customers, demanding creditors, and difficult employees?

- ❏ Do you have the attention to detail that most businesses demand?

- ❏ Can you deal with the bookkeeping requirements of the business?

- ❏ Are you prepared to "eat, sleep, and drink" the business 24–hours a day, 7 days a week (because that's what it frequently takes)?

- ❏ Can you deal with adversity without losing your cool?

- ❏ Can you deal with uncertainty without losing sleep?

- ❏ Are you a good "people person" who can successfully deal with both customers and employees?

- ❏ Can you accept the potential significant financial loss that investing in the business exposes you to?

Of course, you want to keep in mind that in many businesses some of the considerations I've listed above can be softened or even eliminated with the right employees. For example, the accountant/bookkeeper will deal with most of the tedious number crunching requirements, but you'll still have to understand what they're doing and frequently monitor the figures.

After you've considered all of these issues and still feel that small business ownership is for you, then congratulations! Small business ownership can be one of the most financially rewarding and intellectually stimulating pursuits you can follow in life. The freedom of directing your own economic destiny without the 9:00 AM to 5:00 PM grind of the typical boring job can make you really feel alive and excited about earning a living. Imagine actually looking forward to going to "work" everyday!

Alright, if you've gotten this far, you're probably convinced that owning a business is for you, so let's continue on with information you'll need in pursuing this objective.

Sources Of Information On Businesses For Sale

There are many sources of information regarding businesses for sale which should be explored thoroughly. Although this chapter is slanted towards buyers, whether you're buying or selling a business, you should read this chapter. I'll list the major ones here and then discuss the pros and cons of each:

- ***Newspaper classified advertising*** under Business Opportunities

- ***Newsletters*** of various kinds (in-house brokerage publications, regional and national independent publications, etc.)

- ***Business Brokers*** themselves (most reputable ones are listed in the telephone yellow pages and with national and regional professional associations)

- ***Word of Mouth*** through friends, family, and colleagues from all walks of life

- ***Magazines*** and other periodical publications

- ***The Internet*** (but usually not under "business opportunities", but rather, "businesses for sale")

As I discuss each of these information sources for locating operating businesses for sale, I'll provide some specific sources and addresses for you. However, because addresses tend to change over time (especially on the Internet), they may become outdated. At least it gives you a starting point and any good Web search engine such as Yahoo.com or Overture.com will help you even further.

Newspaper Classified Advertising

Classified ads in the Business Opportunity section of your local or nearby major metropolitan newspaper remain as one of the best sources of locating businesses for sale, especially for businesses priced under $1 million. Most newspapers have a particular day of the week that features the most active day for these listings; usually the Sunday edition. Because classified advertising is fairly expensive, most advertisements for businesses for sale don't run continuously. You'll need to constantly scan the listings for a substantial period of time to locate businesses that may be attractive to you. Unfortunately for potential buyers, many good businesses for sale never make it into the classified ads because of the concern on the part of business owners that their customers will learn that their business is for sale, which could hurt business sales. It's more likely that good businesses for sale can be found in the listings in the large metropolitan newspapers (greater anonymity) than in the local suburban - newspapers where no matter how carefully the ad is written, people may determine the actual identity of the business.

One very good way of using the classified ads is to personally advertise as seeking a business for sale and detailing the characteristics of the business for which you're looking. Many business owners who are thinking about selling but haven't formally decided to do so, scan the business opportunity section to get an idea as to what's available for sale and what the asking prices are for similar businesses to help them in their own planning. By advertising for yourself as a buyer, you may be able to find business opportunities available before the general market hears about them and consequently may be able to make a better deal. Some of the large metropolitan newspapers have "businesses sought" or "business wanted" sections that would be a good place to put your ad. Also, keep in mind that many businesses can be relocated. So, if you're looking for this type of business, it may make sense to expand your search fairly widely within your region of the country. Some easily relocatable business types within a region are:

- Publishing
- Distributorships
- Some manufacturing
- Mail order
- Telemarketing
- Export/import

- Consulting (business)
- Consulting (environmental)
- Paging and cell phones
- Vending routes
- Trucking/transportation

Newsletters

There are various newsletter type publications throughout the country that collect various business for sale information to present to potential buyers. The newsletters are usually excellent sources of reasonably up-to date information on a broad array of businesses for sale. These newsletters take the following general form:

1. Local broker newsletters published by individual brokers that list only their listed businesses for sale.

2. Coalition business brokers who combine their listings together in a newsletter format within a specific market area.

3. Regional and national newsletter publishers that combine many listings in a range of categories across regional and national markets.

Since the writing of the first edition of this book, the Internet has substantially replaced the printed regional and national newsletters. However many of the larger brokerage firms still publish their own newsletters for use with their prospective buyers.

Business Brokers

Business Brokers are also excellent sources of information regarding businesses for sale which they represent. Unfortunately for business buyers and sellers, there generally isn't a strong multiple listing service type of collection of businesses for sale as there is for residential and commercial real estate in many parts of the country. However, many business brokers do cooperate together on some basis, and they can always make a particular search for a buyer if a specific type of business is seriously being sought. Your local business broker should always be consulted when you're actively seeking a business for sale. Keep in mind the narrow view that some of them bring relative to the total market. It appears that more and more business brokers are now cooperating together in exchanging business listing information as a result of the ease of information transmission in the modern telecommunication age (especially due to fax, e-mail, and the Internet).

Another drawback with some business brokers is that they are still commercial real estate agents at heart, and may be better versed in selling real estate situations rather than true operating businesses. Many business brokers will be real estate agents by necessity because of the need for a state license to broker the sale of real estate. See Chapter 1 regarding business brokers for a more in-depth discussion of this point.

Word of Mouth

Word of mouth is probably the best way to find out about a good business for sale, but it's also the most unreliable relative to conducting a specific search However, this method shouldn't be ignored. In a way, it's like looking for a needle in a haystack but it sometimes works very well. You just can't sit back and let the information come to you. You should "put out the word" in your business, social, fraternal, and religious circles about your desire to purchase a business. If there are serious sellers in these groups, you may not know about it because of the need for confidentiality regarding a business for sale.

Magazines/Periodicals

Magazines and periodicals are usually national in scope with long lead times for advertising, but they reach a great deal of people. In general, they're not good sources of businesses for sale because most sellers and brokers don't list their businesses in them. However, you should scan the various magazines that specialize in entrepreneurial, business, or financial perspectives such as:

- Inc.
- Success
- Entrepreneur
- Kiplinger's Personal Finance

- Money
- Business Start-Ups
- Small Business Opportunities
- Fortune

The Internet

It's always been a tremendous challenge for buyers, sellers, and brokers of small businesses to efficiently find each other and close the deal. Many would-be business buyers are willing to relocate to anywhere in the country for the right business. Many businesses themselves are not geographic location specific and can be relocated to the buyer's area. Business brokers have many times found themselves in the position of having a motivated and financially capable buyer wanting to buy a particular type of business, but they've been unable to locate the right situation for the buyer. Similarly, business brokers sometimes find themselves with a high quality business for sale but have difficulty finding the right buyer for the business within their immediate geographic area.

The seller of a business may become frustrated with the slowness of the process of finding a qualified buyer and the longer things drag on, the more likely it becomes that word will leak out to employees, vendors, and customers that the business is for sale. Many times this hurts the business operation and ultimately weakens the salability of the business.

The potential buyers of a business generally know their own talents, financial capabilities, and most importantly what kind of business they want to pursue but they quickly become disillusioned when the local business broker and the "business opportunity" listings in the newspaper fail to turn up any viable business purchase candidates.

By my estimation at any given point in time there are approximately 850,000 small to medium sized businesses for sale in the United States. Concurrently, many brokers estimate that they have at least five qualified buyers for every business they have for sale. This means that there are over 4,000,000 buyers spread across the country from Maine to Hawaii right now looking for a business to buy! The logistics of matching the right business with the right buyer has up until now been overwhelming when you consider these numbers. The traditional method of print media advertising is cumbersome, not especially effective, expensive, and is extremely inefficient. If I'm a buyer in Connecticut looking to buy a book distributor anywhere in the country, how do I find what I'm looking for? If I'm a widget manufacturer in California and I know my business can be relocated anywhere, how do I make sure that I find the right buyer who'll pay me the best price for my business without limiting my search to my local area in California?

These problems have now been solved with the advent of the Internet!

Buyers, sellers, and brokers from all over the country (in fact, all over the world) can now quickly and easily find the right situations to match their needs. If you're a business buyer, seller, or broker, and you're not yet connected into this explod-ing business and cultural phenomenon, then you're missing a tremendous opportunity! In fact, if you're a business broker you're in danger of being left behind by your competition. Even if your business objectives are primarily "close to home" in small town America, you should be using the Internet to find and match buyers and sellers of operating businesses. Many business brokers are using the Internet capabilities in their own home towns for strictly local business buyers and sellers, and are finding increased business and dramatically reduced advertising costs.

If you're a buyer or seller of a small business, then the Internet is a gold mine of resources for you to use. Buyers will find that they can obtain information about literally thousands of profitable high quality businesses for sale and sellers will find access to tens of thousands of qualified potential buyers of their business.

Before we go any further in talking about how to use the Internet for buying and selling businesses I'll provide a short primer about what it really is.

The Internet is a sophisticated communication network that uses telephone lines to interconnect computer platforms all over the world. It's a relatively new phe-nomenon having been in existence for use by the general public for only about five years. Although most people now using the Internet are doing so through their computers, it turns out that a computer isn't even really needed. All that's essential is a modem, an input/output device with a keyboard and a monitor (television screen). A whole new industry has grown up around this concept which produces low-cost Internet interconnection devices for use with a home TV. This will only fuel the explosive growth and popularity of the Internet as this new product takes off!

At this time, the vast majority of the estimated 75,000,000 (that's right, 75 million) Internet users are connected to it through modems from their computers. So, if the Internet is this vast collection of interconnected computers primarily using a telephone line as a communications path to connect them, then what is the World Wide Web? Well, in reality, the World Wide Web (I'll refer to it as the Web from now on) is just a part of the Internet. It's a standard that was created in 1991 that makes it easy to access the many different aspects of the Internet. Using the capabilities of the Web, a user can almost "instantly" access an Internet site and download the information contained at that site, including text, color graphics, sound and animation. The Web also established a unique address for every location on the Internet. This address is called a Uniform Resource Locator (URL) and takes the form of http://www.xxxx.com. Just think of this as similar to your postal address or telephone number. You use this address to get to specific sites on the Internet.

Another important feature of the Web is its capability to provide a direct link from one site to another with a click of the mouse or a key stroke. This is extremely important because it allows sites with related information to be easily accessed from each other. Theoretically, a person needs to only go to one location for a particular topic such as "businesses for sale" and that person could be linked from whatever site they enter, to many other sites on the Internet that presents information regarding businesses for sale. That's not yet fully possible today because it now requires each site to cooperate in providing links between their respective sites. While many sites are setting up interactive links between each other, that hasn't yet occurred to any large extent in the "businesses for sale" sites. But not to worry, people looking to buy or sell a business can easily access information about Internet sites that carry the information about thousands of businesses for sale all across the country and even throughout the world by using any of the "search engines" that are available to Web users.

So, the concepts of the Internet and the Web are relatively simple. The Internet is the interconnected communication network, and the Web is the mechanism that allows you to communicate with every site connected to the Internet, including government agencies, educational institutions, and every connected computer in every home and business in the world. Nowadays, almost everyone refers to the Web as the Internet.

There are basically two different ways for you to gain access to the Internet so that you can make use of the capabilities offered by the Web:

• You can use a commercial on-line service such as America On Line (AOL) which will connect you to the Internet indirectly through their site.

- Or, you can access the Internet through a direct Internet connection service provider (ISP). I'm sure that you can find one locally, as they've sprung up like mushrooms in every city and small town in the country. You can also choose to use one of the several national providers such as:

  ◆ EarthLink Network   1-404-815-0770

  ◆ AT&T Worldnet   1-800-288-3199

  ◆ IDT Internet   1-800-375-7431

If you use an Internet connection service provider, you'll need a software application to actually connect your computer to the Internet through the provider's computer. These software applications are referred to as Web Browsers. The two most dominant Web Browsers at this time are Netscape Navigator and the Microsoft Internet Explorer with Explorer being the more popular of the two. These Browsers are software applications that you either purchase separately, as part of an Internet connection package, or which may be supplied to you by your Internet connection service provider or as part of your computer system's software package.

These Browsers can do much more than just connect you to the Internet through a dial-up connection to your Internet service provider. Depending on what you want, they can also provide:

- E-mail capability

- Internet telephone communications

- Security for on-line business transactions

- Creation and publishing of on-line Web pages

- Video, audio and 3D capabilities to allow viewing of the Internet sites with these features

If you use one of the commercial on-line services, you'll also get access to the Internet through them plus you'll have access to many other features that these services offer that you otherwise can't get to. At this writing, AOL is the largest on-line service and is aimed at the mass market (something for everyone).

As mentioned earlier, to actually get yourself onto the Internet to get access to all the great business buying and selling information that's there, you'll need to use an Internet connection software application which is also known as a Web Browser, such as Netscape Navigator or Microsoft Internet Explorer. These Browsers are software application programs that interpret and properly display information that they find on the Web. Because all Browsers use the same basic language, they'll all accurately (more or less) display the same information available on the Internet sites no matter what type of computer or connection device that you use. The main differences are in the way they search for information for you and their ability to display graphics, animation, and sound. These Browsers can now provide video tape quality movies and stereo sound direct to your desktop! But the application of this capability right now is primarily for entertainment and you needn't be concerned with this capability relative to buying or selling businesses.

Once you're connected to the Internet and are using the Web to search for information of interest to you, you'll need to use another innovation called a search engine. Some of the most popular search engines you can use for free and are in use as of this writing are:

- InfoSeek at http://www.infoseek.com

- Yahoo at http://www.yahoo.com

- Excite at http://www.excite.com

- Ask Jeeves at http://www.askjeeves.com

- AltaVista at http://www.altavista .com

- Overture at http://www.Overture.com

You can access any of these search engines for free via an Internet connection. Each search engine searches the Internet differently, but focuses on key words that you enter. Some search engines present you with the most popular sites that meet your criteria, while others use different ways to decide which sites to present to you and in which order. As you use these search engines to find and take you to different sites and you then link from them to other sites you are *surfing the Web*.

I recently selected each of these search engines and had them search for the key words "businesses for sale." I had different results from each one:

InfoSeek returned hundreds of "play per click" sites all advertising businesses for sale. The sites were listed in groups of 15 with 3-line description for each. This is a very good, well targeted web site for the prospective business buyer to search.

Yahoo returned 13,601 site matches but with relatively poor accuracy relative to what I was searching for. The sites were presented in one-line descriptions, grouped in sets of 20, with various categorizations such as:

Chapter 3: Buyers Seeking Sellers

- Business and Economy: Finance:...Business Brokerages
- Business and Economy:Classifieds:Business Opportunities
- Business and Economy:Companies:Franchises:Resources

By clicking on the sites that appeared to be what I was looking for, I was able to quickly visit each site to examine its contents. The only drawback to this is that some sites contain a large amount of graphics and take some extra time to load. Sometimes I had to wait several minutes to have a site load only to find that it wasn't what I was looking for. Examples of this include a business for sale site with just Australian businesses listed and a business opportunity site that sells only get-rich-quick schemes.

EXCITE found 1,816,230 sites with two lines of information for each of the sites. I could search through the top ten sites and then select the next ten sites, etc. Obviously, this much information is too much. I re-did the search using the advanced search feature with which I was able to require that each site have exactly the words "businesses for sale" rather than finding the sites that have any of those three words at all. This time EXCITE returned 54,335 sites. The first 50 sites were specifically related to the information I was looking for.

Ask Jeeves found hundreds of very specific sites relating to businesses for sale and provided 2 lines of very good description.

AltaVista found 30,996,159 sites and presented three-line descriptions for the first group of 10 locations. By using the advanced search technique I was able to get the number of sites down to approximately 1,136,233. Overall, the ability of this search engine to focus in on "businesses for sale" was not as good as the others.

As you have probably surmised by now, the various search engines do their job very differently and how the search is conducted can make a major difference in the results. You'll want to experiment for yourself if you plan to do any Web searches but my experience can be summed up as follows:

- InfoSeek, Ask Jeeves, and Excite (advanced search) seemed to give the best results with a slight edge being given to InfoSeek.

- It's best to take the time to read the search tips provided at each search engine's site before beginning a search.

- It's worth while to take a little extra time to learn how to use the advanced search capabilities, and then use them.

- To do a thorough search for any category, you'll need to use all of the major search engines that you have the time and patience for.

But you don't have to do any search at all to get yourself started! I'll tell you about the results of my searches and point you to the best sites on the Internet for buying, selling, or brokering an operating business for sale.

As I discussed earlier, the problem of matching the hundreds of thousands of businesses for sale in the United States with the millions of potential buyers is a daunting task for any media — except the Web! Many sites have sprung up on the Internet where buyers, sellers, and brokers can exchange large amounts of information easily, inexpensively, and instantaneously. Some of the better known and high quality sites are:

• USBX Listing Exchange	www.usbx.com
• BizBuySell.com	www.bizbuysell.com
• Business Opportunities Guide	www.bizguide.com
• Relocatable Businesses	www.relocatable.com
• MedBiz Market	www.medbizmarket.com
• Business Resale Network	www.br-network.com
• Business Brokers Network	www.bbn-net.com
• Business For Sale By Owner	www.bizsale.com
• BizTrader OnLine	www.biztrader.com

So that you can get a feel for what's available to someone at these sites, I'll describe one of them for you in more detail. Keep in mind that there's no good objective measure at this point as to which site is the "best." Many of the sites bill themselves as "the most businesses for sale on the Web," or "the most visited business for sale site on the Internet." A certain amount of advertising hyperbole is expected in business and the Web is no exception. I've selected the following "businesses for sale" site as a good representative of what you can expect to find on the better sites.

BizBuySell.com is probably the best all-around site on the Internet at the time of this writing for finding information about businesses for sale, buyers seeking businesses, business broker information, and professional associations. Buyers and brokers can find thousands of businesses listed by geographic area from global to country to state/province. By clicking on a particular business category in a particular geographic setting, the buyer or broker is presented with a synopsis of key information about the business for sale that match the search criteria such as:

- Type and Brief Description of Business
- Revenue Range
- Asking Price Range
- Cash Requirements Range
- Country/State/Province Location

If the buyer or broker wants more detailed information, a click of the mouse provides an entire page of details which can include:

- Company History
- Product/Service Description
- Markets and Marketing
- Plant, Facilities, and Equipment
- Company Management
- Company Strengths and Weaknesses
- Growth Opportunities
- Reason For Sale
- Revenues, Asking Price, Cash Required

If the buyer is still interested at this point and wants to know how to proceed further, another mouse click sends the buyer to either information about how to contact the seller or the listing business broker's home page which provides the following information about the listing broker:

- Name, Address, Telephone and Fax Numbers
- Professional Affiliations
- Range of Businesses Represented
- Geographic Area Serviced
- Key Company Individuals and Backgrounds
- Other Relevant Information

The other "businesses for sale" sites offer varying degrees and levels of the information as compared to that which is available at BizBuySell.com. Many of these sites are very worthwhile and you should visit as many of them as you can when doing a search for a business for sale.

I decided to provide this much detail about using the Internet to search for businesses for sale because it has become the most efficient, cost effective way to buy, sell, or broker the sale of an operating business. As a buyer wanting to maximize your selection of businesses for sale, as a seller wanting national (but discreet) exposure of your business, and as a broker seeking to match qualified buyers and motivated sellers together, use of the Internet just can't be beat.

Motivation For Sellers To Sell

Whenever you look at a business for sale, you should approach the situation with a great deal of caution. Someone once said that all business sellers are liars, which is sort of Jungle Law #6, but I don't have sufficient facts to fully back that up. However, you should make it your business to verify all of the information possible about a business for sale. There are some very good motivations for sellers to sell and other ones that aren't so good. Some good motivations are:

- Death of the principal person in the business
- Legitimate retirement of the principal
- Break-up of a partnership
- Serious failing health of the principal
- Spin-off of a subsidiary business for non-financial reasons
- Insufficient access to working capital to maintain or expand a business
- Changing markets, technologies, and the current business owner's inability or unwillingness to deal with the change

Some advertised motivations for sale that usually aren't fully true and that you should be wary of are:

- Divorce
- Relocation
- Other interests
- Burnout

These are generally not good motivations for sale of a business because the problems listed can usually be overcome by the seller without selling the business. It's so hard to get an established profitable business under way, why sell it unless you absolutely have to? You'll probably find it difficult to pinpoint the real reason for sale of the business if it isn't one of the better motivations listed, but it's important that you do so. Knowing what's motivating the seller will help the buyer find the true worth of the business. As a buyer tries to understand the motivation for a seller to sell an apparently lucrative business, the following two laws of the business buying and selling jungle may provide guidance:

Strategic Jungle Law #7:

"If a seller really wants to sell, you probably shouldn't buy!"

Strategic Jungle Law #8:

"Old sellers are the best sellers!"

Buying An Existing Franchise

Although it's true that each business for sale is itself a unique situation with various considerations like no other, some businesses have certain special characteristics that must be considered in addition to the other more standard concerns for all businesses. If you're considering buying an existing franchised business, there are many additional things that must be examined and understood by the potential buyer. For example, some of the most important additional considerations when evaluating an existing franchised business are:

- The terms and conditions of the franchise agreement (contract)

- The royalties, advertising cost sharing, and other fees required

- Conditions and time periods for upgrades of the physical business location

- Approval requirements from the franchiser for the transfer of the ownership of the franchise

The franchise agreement is an extremely important document and should be studied very carefully by a potential buyer. Many franchises are not sold "forever" and they have a specific period of time after which an additional franchise fee may have to be paid or some other condition may be invoked. The buyer should be fully informed about all of the terms and conditions of the franchise agreement before purchasing the business. It may be quite a shock to find out soon after buying the business that the franchise period has expired and that a new franchise fee is required. Typical franchise fees range from $10,000 on up to $150,000.

All costs associated with operating the business relative to the franchise must be understood because many of these costs are variable and may not show up on the current financial statements provided by the seller. For example, royalties are usually paid as a percentage of gross sales but there may be a minimum required. If sales dip in the period of the transaction from the seller to the new owner, the royalty fees may not fall proportionately. Advertising fees are usually assessed monthly, but are sometimes paid annually, and the buyer should determine whether the financial statements present a fair picture of the actual and expected expenses in this area. Also, some franchise agreements require financial participation in unscheduled special promotions decided upon by the franchiser at unspecified times. The buyer may want to determine from the franchiser if any of these special events are planned in the early periods of the new ownership so that proper budgeting for operating expenses can be done.

Another area of concern to a potential buyer is whether there are any required physical upgrades to the existing facilities planned. I once brokered the sale of a well known fast food franchise but the deal almost didn't close because just before the scheduled closing the buyer learned that a major renovation and alteration, complete with new exterior signage, was required to be done within one year. The estimated cost for this turned out to be $50,000, and the business would have had to be closed for at least 30 days during construction work! In Chapter 6 – Conducting Negotiations, I'll discuss how this was handled.

The potential buyer should also determine what the approval requirements and conditions are from the franchiser for the transfer of the franchise to another person. These conditions can sometimes be very strict and may require additional franchise fees to be paid. Surprise! If a buyer is seriously considering buying an existing franchised business, then I recommend that early in the negotiation process, the buyer contact the franchiser not only to determine all of the special operating requirements and costs, but also to determine the approval requirements for the new owner of the franchise. Franchisers usually require a minimum personal net worth, a minimum amount of cash available, certain experience or expertise on the part of the franchisee, etc., etc. It's better to know as soon as possible whether you'll be approved as a franchisee before you and everyone else spend a lot of time negotiating the details of the purchase and sale of the business.

Some other considerations that the buyer should look into relative to their personal outlook and plans for the business are:

- Some franchisers require you to purchase all inventory, supplies, operating equipment, etc. from them or other specified suppliers. (This may limit the ability to lower costs in these areas.)

- Some franchisers require a specific type of location for the business, such as a mall, storefront on a street with a particular traffic count, urban or suburban area, etc. (This may limit the ability to relocate the business.)

- Some franchisers specify minimum operating hours such as 10:00 AM to 10:00 PM, seven days a week for many retail operations. (This may limit your flexibility in cutting labor costs, having free time for yourself, etc.)

Here's a handy checklist that you can use in evaluating the overall professionalism of a franchiser early in your due diligence process:

❑ Find out how long the franchiser has been in the industry and how long the firm has been selling franchises.

❑ Determine how many franchises there are in existence and how many are in your market area.

❑ Determine what the attitude of the franchiser is toward you. Is the franchiser concerned about your qualifications to operate the franchise or are they just pushing you to sign the franchise agreement?

❑ Does the franchiser appear to be interested in a long-term relationship, or just receiving the initial franchise fee?

❑ Learn the current financial condition of the franchiser. Be sure to check the franchiser's financial statements in the disclosure documents. Determine if the franchisees are paying both their up-front fees and their royalties.

❑ Find out the identity of the principal officers, owners and management staff of the franchiser and find out about their background. For example, how much experience in managing a franchising organization do they have?

❑ Compare the franchiser's sales promises with existing documentation. Be certain that their sales presentation is realistic and that any major commitments are clearly written into the franchise agreement.

❑ Verify the franchiser's earnings claims and compare them with other similar business ventures. All earnings claims must be in writing and must describe the basis and assumptions for the claim. They should state the number and percentage of other franchises whose actual experience equals or exceeds the claim. They should also be accompanied by an offer to show substantiating material for the claim.

❏ Determine the legal history of the franchiser. Have any of the executives been involved in criminal or civil actions and is any litigation pending, particularly involving any restrictions on trade that may affect the franchise?

❏ Find out if the franchiser is a member of the International Franchise Association (IFA). If they aren't, ask why not. The IFA has a strict code of ethics that must be met before a franchiser can become a member. Here's how to contact the IFA:

> International Franchise Association
> 1350 New York Avenue NW Suite 900
> Washington, DC 20005
> 202-628-8000 or Fax: 202-628-0812
> web site: http://www.franchise.org
> e-mail: ifa@franchise.org

Turnaround Situations

Although I strongly recommend that buyers seek only profitable businesses with net income sufficient to meet their targeted return on investment, sometimes it makes sense to consider break-even companies or even those that have a negative cash flow, but which are good candidates for turnaround. Occasionally, you may find businesses that are experiencing poor operating results as a consequence of a temporary or easily repairable situation. Some situations that may fall into this category are:

• The recent death of the owner or key business person whom you feel you can replace.

• Extended serious illness of the business owner or other principal person, or other legitimate reason for inattention to the business.

• An apparently temporary fall-off in demand (mild winter for ski resort, cold/rainy summer for lake resort/marina/etc.).

Whatever the cause, you must be more vigilant than ever in verifying not only existing data, but also validating your (or the seller's) premise that the business can be turned around.

Business Location

There are many businesses that may be relocated to your area of the country, so you don't want to restrict your search to just your local newspapers. Some businesses that generally are easy to relocate have been listed earlier in this chapter of the book.

There are also many businesses that can't be relocated under any conditions; but you may want to relocate yourself to the business area. For example:

- A nice quiet "bed and breakfast" inn
- A beautiful ocean or lakeside marina
- Very profitable self-storage businesses and hotels or motels, in rapidly growing areas
- Established manufacturing companies
- Private professional practices (accountants, lawyers, medical)
- Well-established retail businesses
- Existing franchised businesses (a specific location usually must be approved by the franchiser)

Number Of Businesses For Sale

Just how many small to medium-sized businesses are actually on the market for sale? Well, I don't think there's any fully accurate number or complete source of information that anyone can go to for this information. It's even difficult to determine just how many operating businesses there are because of the constant coming and going of businesses and the lack of an accepted definition and categorization of businesses. However, by using various government figures including Small Business Administration (SBA) information, we can get a good feel for what's going on in the field of operating businesses for sale.

A good estimate is that there are about 5.8 million full-time operating businesses with at least one employee in the United States today. These businesses break down into the following categories:

Number of Employees	Number of Businesses
1 – 9	4,600,000
10 – 19	580,000
20 – 49	370,000
50 – 99	133,000
100+	126,000

One way that the SBA defines a small business is by the number of employees that they have. They also have various other criteria including sales volume related to industry type, etc. However, for the purposes of this discussion, the SBA considers businesses with 100 employees or less as small businesses. Using this definition tells us that there are about 5,683,000 small businesses in the United States with the number of employees ranging from 1 to 99.

Based on my own experience and in talking with my colleagues in the business brokerage field, I estimate that there are at any given point in time 10% to 20% of the existing businesses for sale. If I take the mid-point of this estimate, which is 15%, then I can confidently say that at this time there are over 850,000 businesses for sale in the United States. That's 17,000 per state on average and many businesses are relocatable! If you really want to buy a business, I feel confident that you'll eventually find one to suit your needs.

Of course, many of these businesses are very small and may even be home-based businesses in keeping with the recent trends. They may not be profitable and therefore generally not salable, so these businesses may skew the data a bit. But just take a look at the business opportunity classified ads in any major metropolitan newspaper on a Sunday and I think that you'll agree that there are many, many businesses for sale! This is especially true when you consider that the advertised businesses are only a small fraction of what's actually available. The real challenge is to properly value the business once you've found one that meets your criteria and then to negotiate a fair deal so that you can bring the transaction to a successful closing. We've already covered valuing a business in Chapter 2, and we'll talk about conducting negotiations and closing the deal as well as other important issues in upcoming chapters in this book. But first, let's talk about the information you're going to need in determining if you want to buy a particular business.

Key Questions To Ask
A Business Seller

The following are key questions for a buyer to ask a business seller as they investigate the possibility of buying a particular business.

- **Why Are You Selling Your Business?** I've led off with this question because it can be one of the most important ones that you ask a business seller. There are many reasons that a business owner may want to put their business up for sale. Some reasons are good and others may mean trouble for whoever buys the business. You need to carefully get at the true reason for the business sale to keep from making a major mistake.

While there is no one "right" reason for wanting to sell a business, some tend to be better than others and are more apt to not be a ploy to unload a failing business. Some of the better reasons I have run across for wanting to sell a business are:

- *Retirement:* The business owner is elderly, has owned the business for a significant amount of time, and honestly intends to retire and enjoy the fruits of their labor.

- *Poor Health:* The business owner is experiencing significant health problems that are adversely impacting their ability to effectively run the business. Some small business owners live a high stress, fast paced life that frequently leads to serious health problems such as heart disease, as they get older.

- *Death or Incapacity:* Sometimes you'll find businesses for sale that are currently being run by the surviving spouse of the owner/founder/operator. The owner has either died unexpectedly or had a sudden onset of a serious illness such as a stroke that requires that someone step in immediately to keep the business going.

- *Unsolicited Offer:* Some of the best business purchase transactions occur as the result of a buyer making an unsolicited offer to the business owner. Often, these offers are perceived by the business owner to be very lucrative and an easy way to "cash in their chips."

Just as there is no one right reason for a business owner wanting to sell their business, there is also no one wrong reason either. However, in my experience, there are some reasons that should give a potential buyer some concern. Some of these reasons are:

- *Divorce:* This is the most controversial reason as to whether it's a good or bad motivation for an owner of a profitable business to want to sell. Some business brokers have found it to be a good reason, but my experience is towards the negative side of the ledger. If the business is profitable and promising, most spouses will agree to not give up the "cash cow," but will find a way to each share in the proceeds of the ongoing business even if they are divorcing.

- *Other Interests:* Again, this could be a good reason to sell, but it most usually isn't. If the business owner has other interests, why not incorporate them within the context of the current profitable business? This is usually not a good reason for selling.

- *Stress/Burnout:* Although this may be true for the present owner, I wonder if a buyer would want to take on a business that presumably caused this problem.

- *Relocation:* Many businesses can be relocated along with the owner, but if this isn't the case, then you want to find out the reason that the owner needs to relocate. If the business is strong and profitable, that should be an important motivation for the current business owner to not relocate if at all possible.

NOTE: No matter what the stated reason for a business sale, a buyer is cautioned to perform an in-depth due diligence investigation of all aspects of the business before buying. Even the best reasons for sale may be masking some significant hidden problems with the business that will affect future sales and profits. Never forget the old adage; "let the buyer beware."

- **What Are the Last Three Year's Net Operating Profits?** It is very important that you verify for yourself what the last three years of operating profits for the company have been. Of course, you'll need to examine all of the pertinent financial information about the business to accomplish the necessary due diligence required. I recommend that you use only Federal IRS Income Tax Returns or audited financial statements from the business to base your opinion about the business's financial condition. Of course, these documents will not protect you from outright fraud, but they are probably the best information you'll be able to get.

The net operating profit is of primary importance to you because this is the basis that you should use to establish a value for the business. The purchase of a business, in most cases, is a financial investment that must provide an acceptable return on your cash investment to justify buying it and taking the resultant risk. Additionally, the net income from the business must be enough to pay for any debt service that you incur in buying the company. You'll also need to adjust the net operating profit of the business (usually upward) to reflect the unnecessary or "paper only" expenses of the business that can actually be realized as cash to the owner. This is called reconstructing the income and expense statement. The reason you need to ask for three years of financial information is to be able to determine that the operating profit of the business has been sustained for that period of time. You don't want to buy a business based on the last year's profit that may represent an extraordinary one-time occurrence.

Of course, past history of three years is no guarantee for the future. However, most businesses develop sales and earning trends that change relatively slowly, either way, over time. Unless there is a major problem on the horizon (that you should find during due diligence), the typical business should be able to maintain its growth and profitability for the next several years. The minimum information of three years of financial data should be enough for you to make reasonably accurate business operating performance projections for the next few years.

- **Who Are Your Biggest Competitors?** Competition is usually healthy within a given industry because the competing companies indirectly help each other through:

  - Raising public awareness of the products or services offered, thereby helping to create demand.

  - Increasing customer traffic to a particular location, thereby increasing the sales opportunity for all businesses in that location.

  - Incentivizing suppliers to provide cost effective, specialized support to the primary business. And so on ...

For example, it's well documented that increased fast food restaurant competition in a particular location increases business for everyone — up to a point. The early McDonalds franchisees were very nervous when companies like Burger King, Kentucky Fried Chicken, and Taco Bell opened up restaurants on the other three corners of the high traffic intersection that McDonalds had staked its claim to. To many people's surprise, the McDonald's business actually increased as the other restaurants began to attract more and more customers to the area.

So, competition can be healthy, but it can also be deadly for a business. The result of a new WalMart in town helping to put entrenched local small businesses into bankruptcy is legendary. This is why you need to know who the competitors are for the business you are considering buying and what the plans are for any new competitors. This is usually much easier said than done because competitors by their very nature are secretive about their plans and are not about to willingly help you with information. Nor is the business seller usually forthcoming with a buyer about potential competitive threats on the horizon. However, you need to find out as much as you can about future competition for the business you are considering buying. In addition to closely quizzing the business seller, here are some other things you can do:

- If you are considering buying any kind of fixed location retail enterprise, you should check with the local building official to see if any recent permits have been taken out for new locations by potential competitors.

- Read all of the related industry information that you can find relative to the business you are considering. You may be able to find out information about expansion plans for major companies and franchise operators for your area.

- Visit the local Chamber of Commerce, the local and state Economic Development Agency, the SBA's Small Business Development Center, and any other public business/economic organizations to find out as much as you can about any planned business activity in the area that could mean increased competition.

- **What Are Your Industry Trends And Operating Ratios?** Industry trends and operating ratios are very important to consider when evaluating the purchase of a business. The trends will tell you where the marketplace that the company is operating in is heading. The industry ratios will give you a benchmark to compare the company against.

If the industry trend is toward stagnant sales or experiencing a decline, you may want to more carefully consider whether you want to buy into that particular industry. Sure, some people can make money by bucking the trend, but the odds are much better for you if the market trends are expanding for the company's industry. Also, in a declining market you may be able to use this as a bargaining point for a lower sales price with the business seller. A good source of information regarding industry trends is the particular industry association for the business you are considering. For example:

American Assoc. of Ad Agencies
405 Lexington Ave., 18th fl.
New York, NY 10017
212-682-2500

National Auto Dealers Assoc.
8400 West Park Dr.
McLean, VA 22102
703-821-7000

National Retail Federation
325 7th S. NW, Suite 1000
Washington, DC 20004
202-783-7971

Auto Service Industry Assoc.
25 Northwest Point Blvd. #425
Elk Grove, IL 60007
847-228-1310

American Craft Enterprises
21 South Eltings Corner Rd.
Highland, NY 12528
914-883-6100

Auto Parts Assoc.
4600 East-West Highway #300
Bethesda, MD 20814
301-654-6664

Independent Bakers Assoc.
1223 Potomac St. NW
Washington, DC 20007
202-333-8190

National Building Material Assoc.
40 Ivy St. SE
Washington, DC 20003
202-547-2230

National Bicycle Dealer Assoc.
2240 University Dr. Suite 130
Newport Beach, CA 92660
714-722-6909

Indep.Computer Consultants Assoc.
11131 South Towne Sq. #F
St. Louis, MO 63123
314-892-1675

American Booksellers Assoc.
828 S. Broadway
Tarrytown, NY 10591
914-591-2665

Direct Marketing Assoc.
1120 Ave of the Americas
New York, NY 10036
212-768-7277

Of course, the above are just an example of the many industry trade associations that exist. There are literally hundreds of them! You should ask the business seller for the name and address of the specific trade association for the particular business that you are considering to purchase. If the business seller doesn't have this information or you just want to do some preliminary research before talking to a business owner, you should use the Internet to find the association for the type of business you are considering

Industry operating ratios are also an excellent source of information about a business. You should compare the industry averages for the key ratios to the specific ratios for the business that you are considering buying. An excellent source of industry ratio information is:

The Almanac of Business and Industrial Financial Ratios
Published by Prentice-Hall
ISBN 0-13-520503-4
(The information is updated annually)

Key ratios for you to consider are:
- Current Ratios
- Quick Ratios
- Net Sales to Working Capital
- Total Asset Turnover
- Inventory Turnover
- Receivables Turnover
- Total Liabilities to Net Worth
- Internal Rate of Return on Investment

There are many other business ratios that you may want to examine as well to take the operating pulse of the business. Your accountant will be able to help you with this aspect of due diligence if you're not comfortable doing this yourself.

- **What Can I Do To Increase Sales And Profits?** Although it will be your responsibility to bring the business you purchase to higher levels of success and prosperity, the business seller may have some very good ideas about how to do this. Don't confuse this question with an earlier question concerning reconstruction of the income and expense statement. Reconstructed earnings are meant to help everyone to determine today's value of the business being sold and are actual current benefits to the seller (and you, if you buy the business). What you want to learn from the seller before you conclude the sale is what things you might do to increase the sales and profits of the business.

For example, a recent business seller believed that the company's product would be an excellent fit for the new electronic commerce offered by the growth of the Internet. The owner had done some preliminary market research and concluded that for a relatively modest investment, the company's traditional local retail market had great potential to be expanded to the Web. The seller had not bothered to offer this information to the potential buyer because so much of the business valuation discussion had centered on current earnings and historic trends. Besides, the seller figured the buyer had their own ideas and plans in mind. Selling "potential" is always tough because it's impossible to prove.

As another example, an owner and prospective seller of a manufacturing company revealed under questioning by a buyer that an inventor had approached him with a super new idea for a complementary product. The manufacturer produced insect extermination equipment with the principal product line being a generic "bug zapper" that attracted insects by use of a blue light and then dispensed with them through a jolt of high voltage electricity from a fine mesh grid. The new idea was to add an inexpensive, but highly effective female mosquito scent cartridge to the "zapper." The inventor had a patent on this device and documented evidence of a substantial increase in effectiveness. The potential to increase sales and profits for the company could be dramatic if properly marketed. A new and highly effective improvement to an appliance in use in almost every suburban home had the potential of the proverbial "building a better mouse trap."

You must closely question the seller about opportunities that may exist for the business for the future that you would not otherwise learn about if you don't ask.

- **Why Are You Not Implementing The Answer To The Previous Question?** The answer to the previous question logically leads you to this very good follow-up question. If these approaches suggested by the seller are such good ideas, why hasn't the present owner implemented them? There can be some good and some not so good answers to this question. To illustrate this point, I'll refer back to the two situations discussed in the previous question:

  - Expansion of the company's marketing base to the Internet

  - Addition of a great new product enhancement

  In the first case, the seller may not have pursued marketing on the Internet for a very good reason such as his inability to fully comprehend this new technology. Many older people who are faced with the rapid technological advances of the last few years have been unable or unwilling to fully understand the implications of new technical capabilities. They may sense that it will be good for their business, but it may seem like too much trouble to learn a whole new way of doing business this late in their life. So this could be a good opportunity for a new business owner. On the other hand, maybe the seller has had a market feasibility study done which concluded that Internet marketing of the company's product would not make sense. Although a seller is ethically bound to disclose this to you, not all sellers are completely honest (surprise, surprise).

  In the example of the addition of the new feature to the "bug zapper" product, this too could have a good and a bad answer. The owner may say that although he's convinced it's a great idea, the capital costs to purchase the rights to the patent and to retool the product line are too great to be recaptured within the time frame that he has set to begin retirement. In other words, the capital investment will not pay off fast enough and the value of the newly improved product will not be able to be reflected in the selling price of the business. Good answer, and if true, this could be a great opportunity for a buyer with access to enough cash to exploit such an opportunity. But, what if the owner has done a little research and discovered that the benefits of the improvement are illusory? Perhaps the fact that the scent attracts only 90% of the male mosquitoes in the area and doesn't attract the females is a fatal flaw. With all of the male mosquitoes that will escape, there probably is no benefit to the new improved "bug zapper." Other problems could be with approval from the EPA and/or FDA to be introducing a new airborne chemical into our society. Have human toxicology tests been done?

  The moral of this vignette is the old saying "look before you leap." Due diligence is the buyer's responsibility and any claims by the seller of a business as to opportunities for future growth should be viewed with a healthy skepticism. Always check and recheck the facts. Hire professionals in the industry to advise you on the merits of a potential opportunity if you want to be especially careful. But no matter what the potential seems to be, you should only base your purchase price for the business on what it has proven. Don't pay for future income above what the business has shown it's capable of producing now.

- **Will You Hold Financing For The Purchase Of The Business?** Many would-be buyers of operating small businesses are surprised when they realize how much cash they will be required to come up with to purchase the business. Typically, the purchase price for even a small business is in six figures and most buyers are not able to find financing other than loans from their family and friends. Although the SBA is a viable source of funds, that Agency is more likely to fund a business startup than a purchase of an existing company. In many situations involving the purchase and sale of a small business, financing by the seller is the only way to make the transaction occur.

Accordingly, you should ask the seller early in the process whether they will hold financing and under what conditions. Points that you should ask about are:

- the amount or percentage of cash down payment required
- the time frame of the financing
- the interest rate expected on the financed money
- the considerations for balloon payments
- the personal guarantee requirements

Don't be surprised if the business seller wants 25% to 50% cash down to agree to finance the sale. After the seller pays the brokerage commission, capital gains income taxes, professional advisor fees, and other related selling expenses, there may not be much money left for personal reasons such as retirement. It's true that you will be paying the owner a certain amount of money over a period of time, but with very little in the owner's pocket up front, they may be reluctant to finance much more than 50% of the sale price. Sellers will justifiably be nervous about your ability to successfully run the business. If you fail at the business, they may not receive the money you owe them, and there may be no business left to recover.

The time frame of the financing will typically be in the range of five to eight years. Many sellers are retiring and don't want to wait very long to receive the proceeds from the sale of their business. Likewise, you as the buyer should want to pay off the debt as soon as possible so that you can begin pocketing the money that you will otherwise be paying to amortize the pay-off of the purchase note.

The interest rate the seller charges will be at least the going market rate. Don't bother to try to negotiate this lower. The IRS will require the seller to pay taxes on a market rate of interest even if they are not collecting it! Consequently, the seller will most likely insist on a minimum interest rate consistent with the prevailing market no matter what your arguments.

Balloon payments can be used to lower the early promissory note payments to make the business affordable for you. Later, after you have increased the sales and profit of the business, you can either pay off the balloon payment when it's due or refinance it through conventional banking sources.

The seller will most likely require you to personally guarantee all or most of the financed amount. This will help protect their interests in the case of a default by you. This is always an issue of intense negotiation and you can expect to have to guarantee some portion of the financed selling price.

- **Will You Be Willing To Stay With The Business For A Period Of Time?** I believe that it's crucial that a selling business owner agree to stay with the business for a period after the sale to assist in the transition to the new owners. No matter how much you think you know about the business or how much information the seller has given you before the business sale, I guarantee it's not enough. There will be a 1,001 questions that will come up after you get involved in running the business on a day to day basis that only the past owner will be able to answer.

You should negotiate an employment contract with the seller as part of the business sale. Offer the seller a reasonable fee to actually work in the business with you for a three to six month period following the closing. If the seller is unable or unwilling to do this for legitimate reasons, you should at least convince them to take a portion of the sale price of the business in the form of a consulting agreement whereby they will agree to be on call for up to a certain amount of time to assist you with any questions or difficulties you may have. The agreement should specify the amount of time and the duration that the seller agrees to be available to you.

One other way of obtaining first hand knowledge from the seller is to form a temporary partnership with the seller for a period of time before the sale. During this partnership period, you agree to work in the business with the seller for a specified time. You will learn the ins and outs of the business while you are concluding the specific terms and conditions of its sale to you. You may not be surprised to learn that most sellers will not agree to this relationship for many reasons that make good business sense for them. However, you may be able to use this proposal as a bargaining position to get an otherwise reluctant seller to stay with you in the business immediately after the sale.

• **Will You Agree To A Covenant Not To Compete?** It's very important that a seller agree to a Covenant Not To Compete after the business is sold. This is a legally binding contract that stipulates that the business seller will not open a competing business that will affect the operation of the business you just purchased. What a disaster it might be for you if after the business sale is completed, you discover the seller opening the same or similar business right across the street!

Most business sellers have legitimate reasons for selling, such as retirement, illness, or the inability to keep up with a growing business. You probably don't have anything to worry about from them, but you are investing a great deal of money, time, and effort in your new acquisition and it's prudent to legally protect your investment from this type of possibility. The good news is that a business seller with the right motivations will not hesitate to agree to a Covenant Not To Compete. However, if the seller is reluctant or won't agree to such a contract, then red flags of warning should begin flying in your mind.

On the other hand, you have to be practical in the conditions you set in the Covenant. You can't restrict the seller from ever again going into business anywhere in the United States. Sometimes the best-intentioned sellers are bored with retirement and miss the excitement and personal satisfaction that comes from running your own successful business. The Covenant they enter into must allow them the opportunity under certain conditions to open another business. So what are reasonable conditions to expect in a Covenant Not To Compete? Well, the principal conditions will vary from business to business, but in general:

• The Covenant terms should be for a fixed period of time (typically three years).

• The kinds of businesses restricted should be "like or similar businesses." It's a good idea here to define as well as you can what this specifically means. For example, if you are purchasing a restaurant, you may not be able to restrict the seller from having anything to do with the food industry but you can certainly restrict them from opening another restaurant within your competitive area.

- You will need to specify a geographic area for which the Covenant applies. If you are buying a clothing store, then it may be reasonable to stipulate a non-compete area of within 10 blocks in a major city, one mile if you are in a small city, no place within the limits of a small town, etc.

- You should also incorporate language that addresses restrictions not only on the seller acting alone, but also on any partnership or business entity of any kind in which they may have a financial interest.

The key to remember when stipulating the terms and conditions of a Covenant Not To Compete are that they must be reasonable to be legally enforceable and also to get the seller to agree to them. Be sure to obtain professional legal advice concerning this document as well as the other aspects of the business purchase.

- **Will The Business Sale Include Real Estate?** You will need to know if the business includes the transfer of real estate because this will affect your sources of financing and the price you pay for the business. I use the term "transfer of real estate" to cover the major components of real estate that you may have to deal with in purchasing a business:

  - purchasing the business premises from the seller along with the business

  - leasing the business premises from the seller

  - having the lease for the business premises assigned to you if the real estate is not owned by the business seller

If the business seller also owns the real estate that the business operates from, it's usually in your best interest to buy the real estate with the business. An important consideration here will be to value the real estate as an integral asset of the operating business and not separately appraise it according to its "highest and best use." Many times the real estate (location) is extremely important to the success of the business and accordingly, it must be part of the deal. Usually, businesses such as restaurants, retail stores, service centers, and the like are very dependent on their location and you must ensure that you protect your ability to continue to operate from that spot for as long as possible.

There are times that the real estate may be worth more as a separate entity because it can be used for some other more profitable purpose. For example, a restaurant location may be worth more as a site for a condominium development than as a restaurant business. However, if you are buying the business then you shouldn't pay more for the real estate than its value to the restaurant. The restaurant may not be able to exist without the real estate and thus may have little or no value separate from it. The business and the real estate must be considered together as a package even though the actual business sale transaction may be documented separately (deed or lease for real estate and bill of sale for the business assets).

If the seller wants to lease the real estate to you, then you must negotiate terms that are within the operating cash flow of the business. It's also a wise idea to negotiate an option to buy the real estate at a specified price within an established period of time as part of the business sale. You don't want the business seller coming back to you a few years from now after you have worked to expand and improve the business and raising the least terms to a point that eat up all of the increased profits that you've been able to generate, or worse, puts you out of business.

If the seller doesn't own the real estate and is leasing it from a third party, then the best thing to do is to make sure that the terms of the lease are acceptable to you (time period, rental payments, escalation's, etc.) and that it is assignable. Many landlords see the transfer of ownership of a business as a good time to require a hefty increase in rent. If the current lease has acceptable terms regarding the business operation, but it isn't assignable, you may have a problem. Ask the seller to provide you with a copy of the lease to make sure that it's something that the business can operate with.

• **Don't You Have Children To Transfer Your Business To?** This may seem like a strange question to ask, but it's a good one. Almost everyone has children and by the time a business is established, profitable, and the owner ready for retirement, a seller's offspring are usually adults and have to be considered as possible candidates for taking over the business and keeping it in the family. The statistics bear this out as over 50% of the small businesses in the United States are family owned and operated, with more than one generation actively involved. You need to find out why the seller is not considering transferring ownership to their heirs. There are many good reasons why a business seller is not planning to transfer the business to one (or more) of their children:

  • They have no children

  • The children are not capable of running the business

  • The children are not interested in running the business

- The business owner needs a certain amount of cash for retirement or other reasons and the children have insufficient resources

- The business owner and the children are estranged

There is also at least one very good reason why the business owner with adult children is offering the business for sale that is unethical, but sometimes happens. Some business owners who intend to transfer the business to their children are unwilling to pay the fees associated with a professional valuation of their business. They instead list their business with a business broker (who does a market assessment valuation of some kind) and they shop the business around to see what kinds of offers they get. Typically, they will get the broker to take the listing at an exorbitantly high value. Because the price for the business is so high, no one will offer that amount and the seller will not have to sell or pay a contingency-based commission to the broker. The seller ends up with a free market-based valuation of their business that they can use in establishing a buyout price with their children.

Of course, relatively few business owners use this unethical practice and most experienced business brokers are able to weed these faux sellers out before they take a listing. But a few are still able to do this, especially the businesses that are advertised as "for sale by owner." Here are a few of the indications that should make you cautious:

- The seller has adult children and cannot provide a good reason to you why they are not taking over the business.

- The business asking price is set extremely high and the seller seems unwilling to negotiate.

- The business isn't represented for sale by a business broker or other professional intermediary.

- **Are You Looking For A Corporate Stock Or Asset Sale?** Many business sellers want to sell their corporate stock in the company if it's incorporated. If the business is not incorporated and is operating as either a sole proprietorship or a partnership, the sale of the business will be an asset sale by necessity. I usually advise buyers (when I represent them) to try to avoid buying the corporate stock and instead, buy just the assets of the company. The principal reason to avoid purchasing the corporate stock is to avoid buying hidden liabilities associated with the corporation. These hidden liabilities can take the form of:

  - lawsuits arising out of past corporate actions

  - unpaid taxes assessed as the result of future income tax audits for prior years

  - unknown creditors from past years

Technically, you may not be liable for these problems, but the corporation is a legal and enduring entity and it could be held liable. If you are the sole or primary stockholder in the corporation, than in effect you are responsible, at least financially. It is usual in the purchase of the corporate stock of an incorporated business for the seller to indemnify the buyer against any hidden (unknown or undisclosed) corporate liabilities for some period of time. Sometimes in the case of likely liability problems, some sale proceeds will be held in escrow until the issue is fully resolved. But, why subject yourself to these problems if you have a choice? Many times it's better for the buyer to form a new corporation for the purposes of buying all of the assets (both tangible and intangible) of the corporate entity under which the business has been operating. From a business operation, this may not present a problem. The business trade name, trademarks, equipment, real estate, copyrights, inventory, etc. can all be sold to the new corporation. The real estate leases, equipment leases, and franchise agreements can all be assigned from one corporation to another if the business has been properly prepared for sale. You, as the new owner, should be able to take over operation of the business in this way so that it's transparent to the customers.

From a tax perspective (at least as of this writing), there is little consequence to the seller either way, but for you as a buyer, the asset sale may give you an ability to allocate more of the purchase price of the business to depreciable assets — thereby sheltering more income than if you elected a corporate stock sale.

- **Who Knows That The Business Is For Sale?** You'll want to know the answer to this question to understand the extent of damage control that you will have to do after you complete your purchase of the business. In almost all sales of small, privately held businesses, the seller strives mightily to maintain secrecy about the business being for sale for the following reasons:

  - Employees become nervous about their future under a new owner and may "jump ship." If a key employee decides to leave, it may seriously impact the ongoing success of the business.

  - Suppliers become nervous about the usually generous payment terms that they have extended to the present owner based on years of good relationships. They may want to tighten things up if they suspect they will soon be dealing with a new principal in the company.

  - Competitors try to gain advantage of the situation by luring customers away based on the uncertainly about the future of the newly transferred business.

- Customers may be hesitant to continue doing business with a company which is no longer headed by someone they trust and are familiar with.

- The seller's family members may become very nervous about the contemplated sale of the business and the major change in their lives, especially if they hear about the business sale from strangers.

These are all good reasons for concern and for keeping a planned sale of the business as secret as possible, but inevitably the word leaks out in direct proportion to the amount of time the business has been on the market. In fact, the business owner may have already "shopped the business around" by approaching key employees or potential strategic buyers, such as suppliers and competitors. You should specifically and pointedly ask the business seller about who has been approached concerning the business being for sale and who else may know the business is on the market. Of course, all businesses are different and some will not be affected at all by the general knowledge that the company is for sale. There is no rule of thumb to apply here relative to any type or size of business other than to say that in general, the less anyone knows about an impending business transfer, the better, except for the seller's immediate family members. You should make sure that they know about the seller's plans to sell the business well in advance of the closing to ensure that their are no last minute challenges to the sale by disgruntled family members who may feel they have a say in whether the transaction takes place or not.

- **Who Will I Be Negotiating With?** Many business sellers have a bevy of advisors and representatives involved in the planned sale of the business. Depending on the size of the business, there are company accountants and lawyers, business brokers/investment bankers/ergers and acquisition specialists, key corporate management personnel, and maybe a business consultant or two. You need to find out who the decision makers will be and what role the principal will play in the sale of the business.

Often the business owner will set up a "good cop, bad cop" situation for you to negotiate with and the principal will only get involved in the major issues. Of course, you can do this too with your own representatives. The key concept that you want to get straight with the seller after you have made a preliminary agreement in principal is that you want to buy and they want to sell the business. The advisors and representatives, yours and the sellers, can work out the myriad of details, but never lose sight of the objectives: the transfer of ownership in the business.

I've taken some heat for writing in my books and articles that "lawyers are deal killers", but I'll stick to my guns on that. They don't mean to be deal killers, but that's how it will frequently work out if you leave things up to them. They generally have no vested interest in seeing the deal close and they earn their fee either way. They frequently see it as their role to get the best deal for their clients, but the problem comes in that there are lawyers on both sides of the deal. There can't be two best deals, and this is where deal-breaker problems set in. Make it clear with the business seller right from the beginning that all major issues are to be resolved between yourselves and not through the intermediaries. This will go a long way in ensuring that the deal gets done.

• **What Is Your Timetable For Completing The Business Sale?** You need to learn the time frame that the business seller envisions for completing the sale. This will help you in:

    • making your personal plans and adjustments for taking ownership of the business

    • establishing target time frames to arrange any necessary outside financing

    • gaining an upper hand in the negotiation process by using the timeframes to better your bargaining position.

Many business sellers either don't set a specific time frame or set a much too optimistic one relative to the complexity of the transaction. For those sellers who have no specific selling timetable established, you should do everything you can at the outset of negotiations to establish a target date to complete the sale by. Lack of a timetable could:

    • Tend to drive up the professional fees incurred on your part as you work through due diligence and negotiations. Don't forget that time is money where it concerns your attorney and accountant.

    • Indicate that the seller is not really serious about selling the business and may just be trying to gauge the interest for the time the business is really for sale. This could result in an expensive waste of time for you.

On the other hand, if the seller has set a very optimistic time frame, you should not discourage them from this. The short time can be used in your favor to drive negotiations to a more favorable point for yourself. After all, you don't have to buy the business until you are completely satisfied with the terms and conditions of the business sale. The seller may be working to a deadline related to retirement plans (to Florida by Thanksgiving?), a medical problem (upcoming major surgery?), or some other important personal issue (impending divorce?). Just be very careful in your due diligence, because another reason for a short time frame of sale could be a serious business problem on the horizon that may negatively affect the business operations. The seller may be trying to unload before this issue receives general visibility. Although the seller is ethically (and most likely legally) bound to disclose this information to you, not everyone is honest as you may have already discovered.

I've presented you with my view of the key questions that a buyer should ask a business seller early in the potential purchase process. These questions will give you a good sense of the quality and desirability of the business for sale. However, these questions and their related answers and discussion are no substitute for more extensive information and professional advice on this complicated topic. All potential buyers of an operating business are strongly urged to seek competent professional legal and accounting advice during all phases of the process, but especially during the due diligence process and negotiations.

In the next chapter, we'll take a closer look at the due diligence process where I've provided a listing of approximately 125 different items you should consider before buying a business. The due diligence process is crucial to the successful purchase and sale of a business so please read the next chapter carefully.

Usually, at this point, a prospective buyer will enter into an Earnest Money Agreement/Letter of Intent to signify their sincere interest in further exploring the possibility of purchasing the business. Typically, a seller won't provide the detailed information necessary for the due diligence process to be accomplished without an agreement of some kind.

An Earnest Money Agreement, Appendix C (sometimes referred to as a "Letter of Intent") is a document signed by both the buyer and seller that provides the framework for conducting due diligence and negotiating the actual sale of the business. Broad terms and conditions are outlined, the business is described, various rights to be purchased are listed, and any special financing issues are tentatively set forth. To show good faith on the part of the buyer, a deposit of money (earnest money) is provided to the seller or more usually to the seller's representative. This money is usually held in escrow by the seller's broker and is later used as part of the payment for the business at the time of closing.

The amount of earnest money provided by the buyer as part of the Agreement/ Letter of Intent is negotiable and there is no standard amount. Usually, a buyer wants to put down as little as possible, while the seller wants as much as possible. The trick here is to strike a balance that demonstrates that the buyer is very serious about purchasing the business, and by accepting the broad terms and conditions the seller indicates a seriousness about selling. An amount of 5% to 10% of the proposed selling price is typically sufficient to establish a serious negotiation relationship between the buyer and seller. I've included an example of a Binder and Earnest Money Agreement as Appendix C.

I've provided the following handy checklist for you to use in your efforts to purchase a business.

Checklist Of Steps For Buying A Business

❏ Make the decision to consider buying an existing business.

❏ Assess your capabilities and interests to match to a type of business.

❏ Determine the total amount of investment cash you can make available for a purchase. This will include purchase money, closing costs and operating capital.

❏ Focus your search towards a business that matches your skills, experience, interests, and financial capability (your purchase criteria).

❏ Once a candidate business is found, do a preliminary assessment to determine if it meets your purchase criteria.

❏ Enter into a Confidentiality Agreement with the business owner (or business broker) so more detailed information can be exchanged. (See Appendix D)

❏ Enter into a non-binding Letter of Intent or Earnest Money Agreement with a token deposit. (See Appendix C)

❏ Provide the business owner with a confidential profile of yourself, including a resume and your financial resources. (See Appendix E)

❏ Conduct a rigorous "due diligence" investigation of the business. (See Chapter 4)

❏ Negotiate outstanding details (price, terms, assets included, type of sale, etc.)

❏ Enter into a binding Purchase and Sale Agreement with a significant deposit. (See Appendix G)

❏ Prepare all legal and financial transfer documentation and set a closing date.

❏ Arrange any necessary outside financing and assemble your capital resources.

❏ Baseline all variable assets to be transferred (inventory, receivables, etc.)

❏ Close the business sale.

❏ Take possession of the business and begin operations.

4

Accomplishing Due Diligence

- *The Due Diligence Process*
- *Examination and Review*
- *Interviews and Discussions*
- *Confirmation, Verification, and Validation*
- *Calculations, Computations, and Analysis*

What in the world is "due diligence?" I've heard a variation of that question many hundreds of times in my dealings as a business broker, appraiser and as a lecturer on buying and selling a business. I think part of the mystery is in the wording of the phrase itself. The words by themselves don't mean much to the typical person and have more than a hint of "legalese" to them. I define due diligence as:

"The process of investigation by a potential buyer of a business's claimed and actual financial and operational performance."

In other words, it's the process whereby a potential business buyer makes sure that they fully understand everything they can about the anatomy of the company they are considering buying. For most buyers of small businesses, the transaction will be a once-in-a-lifetime experience and the major portion of their financial worth will likely be tied up in the purchase. It will be absolutely imperative for them to ensure to the maximum extent practical that they fully understand the details of the business they are buying. Even more sophisticated buyers, and companies embarking on a merger/acquisition process, must thoroughly investigate the company involved in their purchase plans. Many otherwise very successful companies have been seriously hurt by an ill-advised acquisition! No matter what category you fall into, inexperienced first time business buyer or veteran business operator looking for expansion opportunities, you'll be well served to fully understand and carefully accomplish the process of due diligence. Some of the areas you'll need to consider are:

- The background and history of the company.
- Details about the management and key personnel.
- Information about the primary products and/or services.
- Information about production and purchasing.
- Marketing processes and sales procedures.
- Financial and accounting records.
- Forecasts and pro-forma statements.

The due diligence period tends to have a fairly well defined beginning and an end, although you actually start some semblance of the process the day you begin considering a possible purchase of a company. Additionally, you won't completely stop gathering information and knowledge about the company right up through the actual closing of the purchase and sale. But, there is a formal, well-defined period in which you will accomplish the bulk of the due diligence. This usually occurs in the time frame between when a Letter of Intent is agreed to and when an actual Purchase and Sale Agreement is signed. It's during this time that the company you are considering for purchase should "open its books" to you and may be expected to cooperate with you and your representatives in every reasonable way to satisfy your need to validate their business claims.

Of course, you'll be expected to sign and adhere to a Non-Disclosure Agreement or Confidentiality Agreement before key business information is provided to you. This is a legitimate requirement that the business owner (or their agent) will likely expect you to agree to before any sensitive information is provided. In some cases these Agreements can be very strict with severe legal consequences to you for non-adherence. You can also expect at this time to turn over substantive financial information about yourself. The seller will want to do their own "due diligence" on you to verify that you have the financial ability (or access to necessary funds) to complete the pending transaction, if the sale process proceeds. In fact, you may be asked to pre-qualify yourself as a financially capable buyer before any important business information is provided to you at all.

In this chapter, I'll break down each of the previously mentioned areas of interest and give you a substantial number of ideas about what you should be looking for in your consideration of purchasing a small or mid-sized business. You'll find over 125 specific areas of interest you'll need to consider as part of the due diligence process. I've organized these into four categories:

- Examination and Review

- Interviews and Discussion

- Confirmation, Verification, and Validation

- Calculations, Computations, and Analysis

Please keep in mind that just as all businesses are unique, the actual due diligence process will also be somewhat unique. No checklist or guide will substitute for your own common sense and that of your advisors in attempting to fully understand the nature and makeup of a company that's for sale. You should approach each situation with a healthy sense of skepticism. Take a cue from the slogan of the great State of Missouri; the "Show Me" state. Make absolutely sure that you fully understand all aspects of the business you are considering for purchase, or move on to another opportunity.

The Due Diligence Process

Before I get into the specifics of what kinds of information and knowledge you should be searching for as you conduct due diligence, let's go over the four primary components of the process listed above.

These four components tend to be interwoven in actual practice and may not break out as nicely as they do here in writing. The important point is that you consider each of them as something you must accomplish during the period of due diligence. However, there is a certain logical order to them and you'll find the process easier if you can substantially maintain your due diligence efforts in the order suggested.

You should understand that in most business sales, the information you'll require as a potential buyer is very sensitive to the company under consideration. You'll need to satisfy the business seller that you're a legitimate prospective buyer before any key business information is provided to you. Some of the things that may be required of you include:

- A Letter of Intent (or, Earnest Money Agreement) to purchase the business (sometimes with a non-refundable cash deposit).

- A legally binding, Confidentiality Agreement with specific compensatory remedies for non-adherence or breech of conditions.

- A personal financial statement and other documentation that establishes your financial and technical ability and credibility to purchase the business.

In the *examination and review* part of the process, you should ask for, receive, examine, and review all pertinent documentation and material relating to the conduct of the business. Additionally, you should thoroughly examine all of the physical assets of the company including the office and factory space, the retail space, the inventory, the equipment, and any other tangible asset listed on the company's balance sheet.

In the *interviews and discussion phase,* you should meet with anyone and everyone important to the operation of the business including the owner, CEO, members of the Board of Directors, management, key employees, legal counsel, accountants, etc. Additionally, you should meet with the company's vendors, key customers, bankers, competitors, and anyone else with information about the company that may be of value to you. Understand that these meetings may not always be possible in some circumstances where it's important to maintain strict confidentiality regarding the pending business sale. However, you must determine your need for verification and where necessary, you may have to insist to the seller that you need to have discussions with these key players in the business. I believe a buyer's need for factual detailed information concerning the business's operations generally outweighs the seller's need for confidentiality.

The *confirmation, verification, and validation* part of the due diligence process will require you to seek and obtain independent third-party confirmation of all written material and oral statements provided by the owners of the company to you. For example, you may want to have the company's financial statements audited by an independent CPA firm. You may also want to validate claims of timelines of product delivery, quality, and customer service by anonymously acting as a customer. Here are a few of the things you can do which will be covered in more detail later in this chapter:

- Verify contracts with vendors and customers.

- Verify agreements and assess the overall labor-management relationship with union leaders and other pertinent parties.

- Verify bank balances and financing arrangements with corporate bankers.

- Conduct a physical audit of the inventory and equipment.

Lastly, you'll need to conduct *calculations, computations, and analysis* of the various financial, and other numerical data to determine a reasonableness of accuracy and a clear picture of how this business fits into its market niche. This is an area in which many people will want to involve a qualified accountant with specific experience and expertise in the purchase and sale of a business. Some of the financial areas that should be considered include; the balance sheet, aging of the accounts receivable, acid test ratio, working capital ratio, net worth to debt, and others. The results of your analysis will give you a good picture of the intrinsic health of the business you are considering buying.

Now that you understand the "big picture" of due diligence and the key things you will need to do to determine the true health of a business for sale, I'll provide you with a detailed checklist for you to follow. Keep in mind that every business is different, so no checklist can ever be totally complete. There are also major differences between the many different kinds of companies. For example, manufacturers and retail stores have inventories to be concerned with and service-oriented businesses generally do not. Additionally, some financial aspects are more important if you are buying the corporate stock rather than purchasing the assets separately. I've tried to cover most of the things you should be concerned with, no matter what type of company you are considering and independent of how you plan to structure the sale. Use your own common sense and good judgment (and that of your professional advisors) as you conduct a due diligence examination of the business you are considering purchasing. And don't forget that you may need to "ad lib" as you go along. The answer to one of your questions may suggest another. The results of one piece of analysis may lead to further, more in-depth analysis. A successful due diligence process will ultimately depend on your business savvy, as well as that of your professional advisors.

Examination and Review

The following documentation and information is important to understanding a business. You should obtain copies of:

- ❏ The last three years of business IRS Tax Returns, and/or,

- ❏ The last three years of business financial statements including balance sheets and profit and loss statements.

- ❏ An interim set of financial statements if it is more than three months into the business's new fiscal year.

- ❏ Financial statements for any other companies which the business seller (or an immediate family member) has an equity interest in and which is a customer or supplier or which shares business space/facilities, expenses, employees, or inventory.

- ❏ All open contracts, both for sales of the company's products/services and for its purchase of goods and services.

- ❏ All licensee and dealer agreements.

❑ Any official documentation describing the company, its products/ services, and its key personnel.

❑ Any annual reports, quarterly reports, Form 10-K filings, prospectuses, or press releases.

❑ Listings of the key employees, their position descriptions, and company organization chart.

❑ Copies of employee employment and/or consulting contracts.

❑ A complete listing of the company assets including date of purchase, cost, current condition, and application within the business.

❑ A complete listing of the company's liabilities (if these are to be assumed as part of the purchase), including mortgages and Promissory Notes payable.

❑ A complete listing of all pre-paid items.

❑ All sales catalogs, brochures, and flyers.

❑ Tear-sheets of recent advertising and marketing materials.

❑ The company's out-year marketing, strategic, and/or business plan.

❑ All product specification sheets.

❑ All product guarantees and warrantees. You'll want to determine if there's a continuing potential product and/or service obligation that will pre-date your purchase of the company and for which you'll be responsible for as the new owner of the business.

❑ All patents, trademarks, and copyrights, trade names, proprietary information, and service marks.

❑ The corporate charter, By-Laws, and the last three years of stock-holder meeting minutes (if the company is incorporated).

❑ Stock option plans and agreements, profit sharing and pension plans, retirement plans, deferred compensation plans, and management incentive agreements.

❑ Shareholders list including names, addresses, ownership status and how shares are held.

❑ Contracts or agreements that restrict the transference of shares.

❑ All documentation regarding the acquisition of any business entity.

❑ The Partnership Agreement and any amendments (if the company is operated as a partnership).

❑ Any subsidiary or joint-venture agreement documentation.

❑ Franchise Agreements.

❑ All real estate deeds and leases.

❑ All personal property leases.

❑ All documentation relative to the company's legal ability to do business such as;

  ❑ Fictitious name filing (also known as the d/b/a filing)

  ❑ Sales and use tax permits

  ❑ Zoning and/or Health and Sanitation approvals

  ❑ State and federal licenses and all other government approvals

❑ Any pending and/or settled litigation against the company and/or its officers and management.

❑ All real estate mortgages, promissory notes, and any other long-term debt documents.

❑ Written employment policies and practices.

❑ Affirmative action plans.

❑ All insurance policies.

❑ All collective bargaining agreements, employee stock option plans, and pension plans.

❑ A listing of any labor relations problems and/or disputes including any past work stoppages.

Interviews and Discussion

This part of the due diligence process is sometimes especially difficult because of the secrecy usually required by the business seller. Every business broker can tell you about the seller who demands that; "the business be sold quickly but don't tell anyone about it!" However, as a prospective business buyer, you owe it to yourself to thoroughly examine every aspect of the company. The only way to find out some of this information is to talk with people about it. Keep in mind that there are certain privacy issues that will have to be resolved in order for you to obtain any meaningful information from some of the sources I've listed below. For example, you'll most likely need a signed authorization from the seller before the company's banker will release any information to you. If you're a serious potential buyer with the means to complete a purchase, and the seller is serious about selling, and a Letter of Intent (or Earnest Money Agreement) or similar documentation has been executed, and a strict legally-binding Non-Disclosure Agreement has been entered into, you should be able to have access to any and all information about the company. Here are some of the interviews and discussions you should consider having:

☐ An early meeting in the process with the business owners to discuss the "big picture" views for the company's current operations and future opportunities. Keep in mind there is likely to be a certain amount of hyperbole and puffery involved.

☐ Another meeting with the business owners later in the process to discuss any issues that you may have discovered. It's best that you document all of your questions and concerns ahead of this meeting and provide them to the business owner to allow time for them to prepare detailed answers.

☐ Discuss the employees' perspective of the company with a representative number and cross-section of the work force. It's especially important to talk with the key employees as well as representatives of the rank and file.

☐ Meet with the local leader(s) of any labor unions to verify agreements and contracts and to assess the overall relationship between them and the company's management. A meeting of this nature may have unintended ramifications and it's usually best to have this particular meeting with a member of the company's current management in attendance with you.

☐ Meet with the company's bankers. You'll want to assess the overall financial stability of the company and its creditworthiness (at least in the eyes of the current banker). Find out what lines of credit the company has, how often they're used and their cost. You also want to discuss the company's long-term debt and the potential for transfer to a new ownership (sometimes corporate debt is personally guaranteed and may not be transferred automatically as part of a business sale). The company banker is also a good source for possible information about the overall integrity of the seller. Of course, you'll have to broach this subject in a very carefully camouflaged manner.

❏ Meet with the company's major creditors. You should learn the credit history of the company, find out about any early/on-time discount structures, return history, and get an overall assessment of the bill-paying record of the business. Keep in mind that slow payment of some creditors may not necessarily be bad - it may just be "good business" on the part of an aggressive business owner.

❏ Meet with the company's major customers (if applicable). You'll want to try to find out how long they've been customers, what they like (and don't like) about the company, and attempt to get a feel for their plans after the company changes ownership. Sometimes customers are loyal only to the current owner and they may take their business elsewhere after a sale.

❏ If the company has a large diverse customer base with no "major" customers, you should consider becoming an anonymous customer of the business yourself. Assess the ease of purchasing, the customer service, and any other factors that may provide clues as to the overall quality and customer satisfaction with the business.

❏ Sometimes talking with people in the general community can be helpful to getting a feel for the company's local perception. This can be very important if the company draws its customer and/or employee base from the immediate geographic area. A bad impression of the company may be difficult to overcome (or may be seen as an opportunity).

❏ As harsh and distasteful as this may seem, you may want to also determine whether or not the seller and/or any officer of the company have ever been charged or convicted of any business crimes such as fraud or embezzlement. A visit to the local law enforcement authorities may be a good place to start with your inquiries.

When conducting the meetings and interviews suggested above, you will be much more successful at obtaining the information you need if you have prepared a set of questions in advance. This will ensure that you don't forget anything you want to ask and will provide a framework for moving the discussions along. You can always ad-lib additional questions during the actual interview based on the answers you receive. Always ask open-ended questions that elicit something other than a yes/no response. For example, don't ask; "Do you think this is a well run company?" Rather, ask questions such as; "What do you think about the way this company is run?" "What areas of improvement would you like to see?"

Confirmation, Verification, and Validation

In this phase of the due diligence process you'll want to use all reasonable means to make absolutely sure that all of the business information that's been provided to you is true. You'll never be able to validate and verify 100% of the information you've gathered, but key data should certainly be confirmed. One way to make this part of the process easier is to focus on those aspects of the business sale that are the most important to you. If you're financially motivated, then examine and test the books very carefully. If you're seeking a broader customer base, the validation of the claimed business clientele may be most important to you. If you're only interested in acquiring the business real estate, then close attention to the lease or ownership details should be your primary concern. Whatever your purchase motivations, tailor your information confirmation/verification/validation process to fit your own needs. Here are some steps to consider:

❑ Verify the good standing of the corporation with the Secretary of State in which the company is incorporated.

❑ Conduct a preliminary count of the inventory with special concern for any out-dated non-salable material or merchandise. A final count and valuation will be done just before the actual closing of the sale but it's important to do a preliminary count to determine what kind of issues may eventually arise.

❑ Verify the level of the accounts receivable by confirming amounts with the customers and/or by examining shipping documentation.

❑ Verify that the accounting practices followed are in keeping with similar businesses in the industry (FIFO, LIFO issues, for example).

❑ Verify all open contracts with vendors and customers by confirming the key terms and conditions with them.

❑ Verify that the company is in compliance with all fair labor standards (overtime, child labor, minimum wage, anti-discrimination, etc.)

❑ Physically examine the assets to verify their existence and condition. You may want to hire an outside appraiser to get a valuation opinion.

❑ Physically visit and examine all of the business premises as practical to verify their existence, condition, and application of use. Try to get an idea of whether the primary business space is used efficiently and for the purposes stated.

❑ Have appropriate environmental tests done on all real estate to be purchased as part of the business sale.

❏ Consider having the business financial statements audited by a Certified Public Accountant. This could be an expensive option but may be important to do in large transactions and/or companies with multiple sites and operating divisions.

❏ Examine the industry in which the company operates with a view to determining trends which may affect the future of the business:

   ❏ Learn about new developments in the industry by reviewing trade publications. Is the company you are considering on the leading or trailing edge of innovations in the industry?

   ❏ Determine the overall industry size and growth rate. A relatively small industry size with a declining growth rate may signal trouble for the company you are considering.

   ❏ Determine whether the industry is susceptible to cyclical influences. Make sure that you're not buying a business in an industry heading into a major down cycle.

   ❏ Assess any seasonal effects on the company. This may not be a major concern when looking at the long run, but it may dictate that you have more operating capital in the near term than you will need on average throughout the year. For example, buying a Christmas-oriented gift shop in the spring or a lawn products manufacturer in the fall may have cash flow implications.

   ❏ Evaluate the overall short and long term prospects for the industry and relate these to the company's growth potential.

   ❏ Compare the company's past business plan with the results achieved. This may give you an insight into management capability and company health.

   ❏ Examine the demographic and geographic markets in which the company sells its products and/or services. Try to assess whether these markets are changing and if so what effect it is likely to have.

Most businesses have some negative feature(s) that the sellers will sometimes not want to disclose. You must do everything you can to find out what these are and factor them into your decision as to whether to buy the business. There are many possible problems with a business and some examples of these include:

   ❏ Credit problems with banks and/or suppliers.

   ❏ Personal matters pertaining to the seller that may affect the owner's ability to sell the business (e.g., divorce, legal proceedings, etc.).

❑ Recent bad publicity, and/or bad reports at the Better Business Bureau, the Chamber of Commerce, etc.

❑ Expiring patents, licenses, copyrights, etc.

❑ Changing franchise terms that will increase operating expenses or degrade future business opportunity for the company.

❑ An impending or actual real estate zoning change that will make business expansion difficult or impossible.

❑ Major new competition being planned (such as a new shopping center or a new mega store in the area).

❑ Increasing difficulty or expense in obtaining raw materials, products, or services necessary to the operation of the business.

❑ The potential non-renewal of a major sales account.

❑ Significant increases in rent or other changes to the lease terms to be expected (if the business space is leased).

❑ Unapproved existing variances in violation of zoning regulations.

❑ Leases that are non-assignable or non-renewable.

❑ Legal claims, encumbrances, or liens against the business.

❑ Pending litigation against the company that have the potential to impact future business.

❑ State and/or federal law violations that will require a major expense and/or difficulty to correct.

❑ Poor management of capital assets such as major equipment and real estate that have eroded their value and/or usefulness.

❑ Obsolete machinery and/or overvalued inventory.

❑ Partner(s) and/or shareholder(s) who may not concur with the seller's desire to sell. You must verify that company can legitimately be sold before you invest significant amounts of your time and efforts.

❑ Unpaid taxes (income, sales, FICA).

❑ Product obsolescence or failure to keep up with technological changes.

❑ Potential major increase in product liability insurance.

❑ Potential labor union or other employee related problems.

❑ Inability of a buyer to replace a "superman" seller who has a unique capability for running the business.

❑ Non-compliance with environmental and/or safety requirements.

❑ Recent suspension of a liquor license for regulation violations.

❑ Need to hire law enforcement to handle rowdy customers at certain times (movie theaters, nightclubs, sports arenas, etc.)

❑ The business having any stigma associated with violent crime, drug abuse, pornography, communicable diseases, or similar ills of modern society. This may sound distasteful but a due diligence process should ensure that none of these kinds of problems are impacting the business for sale.

Calculations, Computations, and Analysis

This last phase of the due diligence process involves much more than the confirmation, verification, and validation of business information as discussed previously. In this phase you should be able to determine the true business pulse of the company you're evaluating. Determine not only how well it's doing within its own operational scope, but how well it fits into its market niche. From this information you will be able to make informed judgments about the future of the company that may or may not fit your goals relative to the purchase of the business. Don't ever forget that in reality, no matter what your basic business motivations, you're buying future results, not past performance. Here are some things you can do that will provide guideposts you can use to extrapolate past and current performance into realistic future expectations:

❑ Conduct a balance sheet test. Take current assets (the cash on hand and in the bank) and accounts receivable and divide the amount by the current liabilities. The ratio should be 1.5 to 1 or better in favor of the assets. However, a business owner may be running a "lean" operation in anticipation of a sale. A ratio of 1 to 1 is the minimum you should expect in an otherwise healthy company although there are certain exceptions in very small businesses such as retail stores.

❑ Determine the age and history of the accounts receivable. Current receivables are 30 days or less old, potential problem receivables are 60-90 days old, and any receivable over 90 days on the books may not be collectible. Be sure to look at the accounts receivable history for at least a year. Sometimes sellers "clean-up" their receivables in anticipation of offering their business for sale.

❏ Conduct an acid test ratio. Take the cash and net receivables and compare them to current liabilities. A solid business will have a ratio of at least one to one. That is; there is enough cash on hand to meet the current liabilities. This will also give you an idea of how much additional cash you'll be required to provide as part of the working capital after you complete the purchase.

❏ Do a working capital ratio test. Take the cash (and cash equivalents), accounts receivable, inventory (finished and in-process), add them up and subtract the current liabilities; the result is the working capital (the money available to expand business operations). The real value in this ratio is to compare it to several past years. If working capital increases, that's good. If it's decreasing, that may indicate a problem with the business that you'll want to investigate further!

❏ Calculate the net worth to debt. If there is an excess of net worth over total liability this may indicate a healthy company. If the reverse is true, the business may have a negative value and perhaps be the reason it's being offered for sale.

❏ It's always helpful to calculate and evaluate the company's gross and net profit on gross sales. The net profit margin is the gross sales as compared to the net income. Both are usually expressed as a percentage. The gross profit margin in a healthy company is frequently 60% or higher with the net profit margin 10% or higher. Of course there are many exceptions to this and it's best to compare the particular company operating result with similar companies in its industry.

❏ Many financial analyses are important to consider over a period of time rather than as the result of a one-time snapshot. It's best to evaluate financial performance over at least a three year period to get the best view of performance. For example:

   ❏ Is the working capital position increasing or decreasing?

   ❏ Does the acid test show improvement over time, or not?

   ❏ Are the accounts receivable rising relative to current assets?

   ❏ Are the accounts receivable rising significantly in relation to total sales? If so, this could mean that higher credit risks are being taken by the owners to show an improved sales picture.

   ❏ Is the inventory turnover improving or not?

❏ There are many other financial ratios and averages that you can also check to help you get a good feel for the overall health of the company. You should compare as many of them as possible to the industry averages for this particular type of company. A good source for information about industry financial ratio averages is the Almanac of Business and Industrial Financial Ratios (updated annually) and published by Prentice Hall. Some of the financial data they provide for almost 200 industries broken down by the size and profitability of a company are listed below. This set of data makes a good financial due diligence check-off list in itself:

- Net Sales
- Total Revenues
- Cost of Operations
- Rent
- Taxes
- Interest
- Depreciation
- Pensions
- Officers Compensation
- Operating Margins
- Net Receivables
- Inventories
- Property, Plant and Equip.
- Total Assets
- Notes and Loans Payable
- Net Worth
- Asset Ratio
- Quick Ratio
- Net Sales to Working Cap.

- Coverage Ratio
- Total Asset Turnover
- Inventory Turnover
- Receivables Turnover
- Total Liabilities to Net Worth
- Debt Ratio
- Return on Total Assets
- Return on Equity
- Profit Margins Before and After Income Tax
- Cost of Payroll
- Average Net Receivables
- Average Inventories
- Average Net Worth
- Return on Assets
- Return on Equity
- Total Liabilities to Net Worth
- Operating Leverage
- Financial Leverage

❑ Using the past (and current) financial information, provide your own financial forecast for the company (a pro forma) for at least the next year after you purchase it. Be sure to calculate your own working capital needs and compare those to your available financial resources. In many business sales, all of the current assets are taken by the seller (and current liabilities paid off) but this will require you to provide net working capital in addition to paying the negotiated purchase price of the business (which may involve a substantial up-front cash payment).

❏ You should do your own reconstruction (recasting, normalizing, etc.) of the company's profit and loss statement to determine the actual available cash flow that will be available to you for business operations (including purchase debt payoff). Typically, the seller (or more likely the seller's business broker) will provide this as part of the descriptive sales package for the business. Use it only as a starting point for your own reconstruction based in part on the results of your due diligence findings. Invariably a seller's reconstructed earnings are much too optimistic.

❏ Do an analysis of the company's spending on research and development. For manufacturing companies a healthy figure is about 5% of gross sales. Determine if the actual R&D spending has been increasing or decreasing in recent years. Frequently, companies will cut back R&D spending in the year or two before the company is put on the market for sale to boost the net operating profit. Assess whether the company's future prospects have been impacted by any strategy of this nature.

❏ Develop your own strategic analysis of the company and its operations. Consider not only how the company does things now but what positive impact you could have as a new owner.

❏ What are the long-range goals of the business?

❏ How does the business measure success?

❏ What are the key strengths the business uses for success?

❏ What are the most important weaknesses in the business?

❏ Are there current opportunities within the company or industry?

❏ What are the biggest risks that the company faces?

The process of due diligence is crucial in evaluating a business for sale and perhaps as you can tell from this chapter, it can be quite complicated. There is no substitute for basic common sense on your part, a solid understanding of general business principles, and the advice and guidance of qualified professionals in the legal, accounting, and business brokerage fields. You are well advised to read all you can to learn as much as possible about the process and to select highly qualified advisors to assist you.

Sellers Seeking Buyers

- *The Best Time To Sell A Business*
- *Preparing A Business For Sale*
- *Deciding Whether To Use A Business Broker*
- *Buyer's Financial Qualification Statement*
- *Types Of Potential Buyers*
- *Facing The Issue Of "Holding Paper"*
- *Checklist Of Steps For Selling A Business*

Deciding to sell your business may be one of the most important decisions you'll ever make and probably the hardest. When business is good, your income ample, your work interesting and the future appears promising, you may ask yourself, "Why sell?" Some reasons may be retirement, a decline in health, the desire for more free time, the situation of not having an heir, partner problems, or a decision to relocate.

The Best Time To Sell A Business

Simply stated, the only time a business can be sold for a favorable price that will enable a seller to realize the highest return on their investment of time, money, and sweat equity, is when conditions surrounding the business are strong and the future is promising. When you sell your company, you're in a position to realize at least three important benefits. First, the sale will allow you to eliminate the risk and uncertainty associated with small business ownership. Second, the sale converts the equity and goodwill you presently hold in your company into cash. Cash in itself delivers a third benefit, namely, that you'll be in a position to pursue new and alternative opportunities in both your business and personal life.

Preparing your company for sale is almost as important as the sale itself! You'll sell your business only once, therefore you'll want to plan for it very carefully. Getting the best price for your business is not simply a matter of "driving a hard bargain." Numerous factors must be considered in addition to your readiness to sell, including the money market, buyer's interest level, the current profit levels in your trade or industry, how your business is presented, and how the sale is structured.

In the previous chapter, I estimated that there are at least 850,000 small operating businesses for sale in the United States at any given point in time. This is a significant number of opportunities for buyers to evaluate and these numbers require that you position your business in its best light to attract the attention of serious, qualified buyers. How many businesses for sale actually sell rather than go out of business and are dissolved? This is also a difficult number to determine with any accuracy, but based on my experience and that of other business brokers, I estimate that only 20% to 25% of businesses for sale actually sell, at least in the first timeframe they are offered for sale. Why is this? Well, there are many reasons. Here are a few for you to consider as you think about offering your business for sale:

- The asking price is unreasonably high.

- The selling terms aren't suitably flexible.

- The operating history of the business is erratic or declining.

- The profits don't support a purchase of the business.

- The business revenue and other operating data can't be substantiated.

- The business no longer provides a product or service that's fully supported by the customer base.

- The physical plant and/or equipment has deteriorated too badly to justify replacement.

- The sellers change their minds (for any number of reasons!).

In the next section of this chapter I'll discuss preparing your business for sale. If you approach the issue of selling your business early enough (one to two years prior is the best time frame) and properly position the business operations in a way that best demonstrates the value in your business, you should be able to identify a suitable buyer.

Preparing A Business For Sale

The first thing you'll want to do if you're a business owner contemplating selling your business is to prepare it for sale. Don't forget, most buyers will be basing their purchase price for your business on a capitalized value of your available cash flow. Your assets such as inventory, equipment, real estate, etc., don't mean much of anything if your business isn't making money!

This preparation should take at least a year (if you have the luxury of time) to maximize the sales picture and minimize the expenses. However, I'm not advocating doing anything underhanded or misleading. Most business owners get a little sloppy as time goes on, and don't pay as close attention to business details as they did when they first started out. Let's talk about some of the things that you can do to better position your business for sale:

- In the year or two before you put the business on the market, do an aggressive sales campaign to build up your sales picture. Call those old customers/clients and resurrect them as active customers. Run some special sales to attract new customers. The goal is to increase your sales figures without a significant increase in your costs. You don't take any unreported cash sales out of the business, do you? If so, you may want to stop this practice to improve sales and profits. I advise buyers to ignore any claimed unreported cash sales by the seller of the business because they can't be proven. Also, if you admit to a buyer that you're cheating the IRS, how's the buyer going to trust you?

- The most fertile area is probably in the expenses. Do you still have your non-productive relative on the payroll as a favor to some other family member? Most good business brokers and appraisers can reconstruct an expense sheet to "recapture" unnecessary but legitimate expenses for the purposes of improving the net profit for increasing the sale price of your business. The seller should take a hard look at those other expenses that could be eliminated. For example:

  - Unread periodical subscriptions, unused fraternal memberships, outdated advertising, etc. Some businesses are able to "find" thousands of dollars this way.

  - Company vehicles used mostly for personal reasons

– Unnecessary "business" trips to vacation areas for conventions, sales meetings, etc.

– Any other expenses of a personal nature that tend to creep into the checkbook of the small, closely held business

For more detailed information on this subject, please refer back to Chapter 2 which describes how to reconstruct the Income and Expense Statement. The following information may give the seller some other good ideas on how to position the business for sale:

- Bring your inventory up to date with only good salable merchandise by clearing out old stock through special sales or other incentives. The buyer generally won't buy tired old inventory, so you might as well convert it to cash. It'll also increase the revenues for the business which in turn, may improve the overall value of the business.

- Freshen up your accounts receivable by going after those old receivables that have been hanging around. Usually, any normal 30-day account that is more than 90 days old may be a problem. Consider offering the slow paying customers incentives to get their accounts current with you. If you do this during the year before you offer your business for sale, you'll generate additional revenues that will enhance the valuation of your business.

- As harsh as it sounds, this is probably a good time to take a long hard look at your work force. Consider replacing any problem, high-paid employees at lower salaries, if possible. Are all of the employees really needed? The year or two before you plan to sell is the best time to downsize your work force if it has become out of proportion to your business revenue. Obviously, if the same amount of sales can be generated by a smaller work force, then the business profitability goes up and therefore, the overall value of the business goes up when it comes time for you to sell.

For those of you who wish to learn more about preparing a business for sale to sell for the most money, I recommend my book, "Preparing Your Business for Sale," Russell L. Brown, ISBN 0-9657400-1-3. In it I provide you with hundreds of strategies, tips, ideas and other information to help you to unlock the super-money value in your company. You can find the book online at www.BusinessBookPress.com, order it from your favorite book store, or use the order form provided in the back of this book.

Deciding Whether To Use
A Business Broker

One of the many significant decisions a business owner who wants to sell their business has to make is whether or not to hire a business broker to represent them in the sale. In Chapter 1 of this book, I discussed different aspects of what a business broker is and does. You should read that chapter thoroughly before deciding whether to "do-it-yourself." There are some other things that a business owner contemplating selling their business should keep in mind. A very important consideration for most business sellers is maintaining confidentiality that their business is for sale while at the same time offering their business for sale to the widest possible group of qualified buyers. This is frequently a serious contradiction in objectives. These are two key points that bear some further discussion; maintaining confidentiality and finding qualified buyers.

Confidentiality is extremely important to most business sellers for many different but very valid reasons:

- Knowledge that the business is for sale could give an unfair advantage to competitors.

- Potential customers may shy away from doing business with a company that's for sale for fear that policies may change with new ownership.

- Employees may become uncertain about their continued employment prospects with new ownership.

- Inquiries from many unqualified potential buyers ("lookers") may distract the business seller from continuing the normal business operation during the selling period.

- Suppliers may become concerned with their continued relationship with the company.

One of the processes that professional business brokers use to ensure confidentiality is to have prospective buyers sign a Confidentiality Agreement before the name of the business and any sensitive financial information is disclosed to them. I've included an example of a Confidentiality Agreement as Appendix D for your reference. This will go a long way in helping to maintain the confidentiality of the fact that your business is for sale and to safeguard your private financial information. You'll definitely want to use an agreement of this kind if you're selling the business yourself. Make sure your broker uses something similar if you're listing with a business broker.

Of course, nothing is for sure, and when you do decide to put your business on the market you should anticipate that eventually it will become generally known that your business is for sale. It may be prudent to privately inform those you most fear will have a negative reaction about the business being for sale, before you actually put your business on the market. You may want to discreetly inform your key employees, suppliers, creditors, and key customers of your intention, to allay their fears right up front before they hear things through the "grapevine." In fact, many businesses are actually sold to customers, suppliers, and employees. Next to you, they probably know your business the best!

The other key point to be thought about when considering whether to use a business broker is the difficulty of finding qualified buyers. A qualified buyer is someone who is ready and able to buy a business such as the one being offered for sale.

A ready and able buyer, i.e., a qualified buyer is:

- Someone who is honestly looking for a business to purchase (there are many nosy "lookers")

- Someone who has the motivation and personal commitment to purchase a business (many people lack the intestinal fortitude to proceed with an investment of the size and associated risk required to buy a profitable operating business)

- Someone who has the financial resources (or access to them) to consummate the purchase

- Someone who has the "right" motivations (e.g., you don't want sensitive business information being given to one of your business competitors!)

If you can't properly qualify a potential buyer, you'll be wasting a great deal of your time. Which brings me to the next law of the jungle:

Strategic Jungle Law #9:

"99% of potential business buyers never buy a business!"

This alone may be reason enough to retain a business broker to represent you in selling your business. A professional business broker knows how to sort through the many non-qualified buyers to get to the few who actually do have the means and motivation to buy a business. However, once the unqualified potential buyers have been culled out, somewhere around 50% of qualified buyers eventually do buy a business.

For many reasons, I strongly recommend that sellers use a professional business broker to represent them in selling their business. A true professional business broker can provide:

- Assistance in maintaining confidentiality of the business for sale by acting as an intermediary

- Assurance that only qualified business buyers are introduced to the seller

- Assistance in positioning the business so that it's seen in its best light

- Targeted, effective marketing of the business for sale

- Assistance in determining the market value of the business

Buyer's Financial Qualifications Statement

At the time that a potential buyer is asked to sign a Confidentiality Agreement, it may also be a good time to ask them to fill out a Buyer's Financial Qualification Statement. It's usually not very easy to get this in such an early stage in the process of potentially buying the business, but it's worth a try. If it's determined that the buyer is not financially qualified to buy the business, a great deal of wasted time on everyone's part will be avoided. One strategy that the seller/broker can use in asking the potential buyer to fill out the Statement is that it's only a reciprocal exchange of sensitive financial information between business parties; the seller provides the business IRS Tax Returns and other financial data to the buyer, and the buyer provides pertinent personal financial data to the seller. Whether or not this is done at this time, it'll most likely have to be done at a later point in the negotiations if the seller is going to hold a promissory note as part of the business sale. I've included an example of a Buyer's Financial Qualification Statement as Appendix E.

Types Of Potential Buyers

Let's talk about two general types of potential buyers that you can expect to encounter in the market place. It's important to know who you're dealing with because some buyers are motivated somewhat differently than others. The two basic types of buyers are:

- Private (approximately 75% of all business buyers)

- Corporate (approximately 25% of all business buyers)

Private buyers are generally considered financially motivated buyers while corporate buyers are considered strategic buyers. Strategic buyers may have reasons for buying a business other than immediate financial income and tend to pay higher prices for a profitable operating business.

The majority of private buyers fall into four main categories:

- Individual

- Partners

- Husband/wife teams

- Employees

Corporate buyers generally fall into the following different categories:

- Related business interests (your competitors?) seeking a larger business base

- Diversification seekers

- Existing suppliers to the business

- Customers of the business

There are many different reasons that private individuals buy businesses with the predominant reason being the most obvious: to make more money. However, there are several other important reasons:

- Buying a job to earn a living

- Acquiring an attractive lease or other real estate (this relates to making money)

- Buying prestige (many business owners are respected community leaders)

- Eliminating competition (relates to making money)

- Buying a hobby or retirement occupation

- Seeking self-fulfillment

- Seeking an opportunity for a child or other family member

If you can accurately determine a particular buyer's motivation, you may make it much easier on yourself in actually selling the business, and you may get a better price as well. If you think that you know what's motivating the potential buyer, then you should focus your emphasis on that motivation during the negotiation process.

Facing The Issue of "Holding Paper"

No matter whether you like the idea or not, you as the business seller will most likely have to take a promissory note ("hold paper") to complete the sale of your business. I know most sellers just want to sell their business and be done with it, but it usually doesn't work like that with small businesses. Unless your business is extremely profitable, very well established, has a strong, consistent, and loyal customer base in a growing market, most banks and other lending institutions will loan only a relatively small portion of the business value, if anything at all. This is especially true if a significant portion of the business value is in "goodwill." In fact, many lending institutions won't loan more than 70% of the fair market value of the tangible assets, and won't loan any portion of the goodwill. So, unless your buyer is extremely well-heeled (has lots of cash), you might want to think about how much, and under what conditions, you'll take back a promissory note against the sale of your business.

Some other thoughts that you should consider on this topic of seller financing are:

- Most sales of small closely-held businesses are primarily financed by the seller. Some business brokers estimate that at least 75% of all small businesses sold involve the seller "holding paper" to one extent or another.

- Most business buyers don't have the entire amount of the business selling price in cash. There are also many other demands for the buyer's money at the time of transfer of ownership such as professional advisor fees, transfer taxes and related expenses, and operating cash requirements to name a few. The buyer will also want to hold a certain amount of ready cash in reserve to cover any surprise expenditures and other contingencies.

- Even if the buyer has the available cash at their disposal or is able to obtain outside financing, they'll usually want to see a continued financial involvement on the part of the seller. This serves to establish some confidence on the part of the buyer that the sales and profitability claims made by the seller are true.

- It's very difficult to obtain third party financing for the purchase of an operating business. Commercial banks, venture capitalists, and other sources of funds are very wary of financing a transaction of this nature because of the many things that can go wrong under a new owner. Most of the potential problems are to extremely difficult to evaluate before the sale of the business. Accordingly, any outside financing may carry such a high interest rate to cover the risks involved that the debt load may make the purchase impossible.

- A seller will usually receive the highest price for the business if they provide the financing for the buyer because they can provide the best terms. The seller has a great deal more latitude in selecting an interest rate and a payoff period than a conventional lender, and consequently will be better able to ensure that a successful sale of the business takes place at the highest reasonable price.

- Because almost all elements of a promissory note from the buyer to the seller will most likely be negotiable items, I'll defer further discussion of this topic until the next chapter that deals with "Conducting Negotiations.

If You've Decided To Do-It Yourself

If you've decided that you want to go it alone and try to find a buyer for your business without the assistance of a professional business broker, a good place to start looking for a buyer is on the Internet. I've provided a detailed discussion of this in Chapter 3. In case you skipped it you should be sure to go back and read it. Many of the "businesses for sale" sites on the Internet offer free listings for business sellers and you're sure to be contacted by many potential buyers as well as business brokers trying to entice you to list your business with them. Although you'll have a good deal of exposure for your business for free, be careful that you don't become overexposed. Most business sellers want to maintain the confidentiality of their business being for sale and this will be very difficult to do in any media if you don't have an intermediary.

Finally, I've provided a handy checklist of steps you'll need to take to sell your business.

Checklist of Steps for Selling a Business

❑ Make the decision to sell your existing business. Make sure you've considered all the personal and financial ramifications.

❑ Assess the overall performance of your company and take actions to enhance/maximize the provable bottom-line profits. This may take some time so get started well in advance of your target time-frame for the sale.

❑ Identify the type of buyer most likely to buy your business and a probable method of sale (asset vs. stock, financing vs. all-cash, etc.). Establish a time-frame within which you wish to accomplish the sale.

❑ Accomplish an appraisal of the potential fair market value of the business. It's best to do this right after the close of your latest fiscal year when all financial information is current.

❑ Assemble a team of professionals you wish to assist and advise you in the sale (e.g.; an attorney, accountant, and business broker).

❑ Enter into a Listing Agreement with a professional intermediary and participate in the showing of the business to prospective buyers.

❑ Receive a profile of the prospective buyer, including their business experience resume and financial resources and a Confidentiality Agreement.

❑ Enter into a non-binding Letter of Intent with a good-faith deposit.

❑ Cooperate with a prospective buyer's "due diligence" investigation of the business. Verify the personal/financial claims of the prospective buyer.

❑ Negotiate outstanding details (price, terms, assets included, type of sale, post-sale seller's employment contract, etc.).

❑ Enter into a binding Purchase and Sale Agreement with a significant deposit.

❏ Have your professional team prepare all legal and financial transfer documentation and set a closing date.

❏ Baseline all variable asset values to be transferred (inventory, receivables, etc.) and comply with the Bulk Sales Law (requirements vary by state; usually a 30 day notification period to your creditors is required).

❏ Close the business sale and turn over possession of the company.

❏ Complete all contracted post-sale actions (employment contract, etc.)

Conducting Negotiations

- *The Three-Step Negotiation Process*
- *Essential Information Buyers Need*
- *Finding The Skeletons*
- *Key Factors In Negotiation*
- *Binder And Earnest Money Agreement*
- *Identifying Rights To Be Assigned*
- *Structuring The Business Sale*
- *Covenant Not To Compete*
- *Seller Consulting Contract*
- *Financing Considerations*
- *Seller Financing Considerations*
- *Working With The Deal Killers*
- *Handling Buyer/Seller Anxiety*
- *Counteroffers*
- *The Purchase And Sale Agreement*
- *Why Some Businesses Don't Sell*
- *Additional Considerations For A Franchise*

There are always two sides to every business buying and selling transaction (the buyer and seller) and a great deal of sideshows (the lawyer, the accountant, the business broker). You should remember this: the buyer and the seller are natural adversaries – the seller wants as much money as possible, and the buyer wants to pay as little money as possible. Whether you're a buyer or seller, you need to find common ground. Other noteworthy factors other than money are also at play in this process, such as:

- Ego (Both the seller's and the buyer's egos need to be considered)

- Time (E.g., failing health or retirement plans on the part of the seller, impending job loss on the part of the buyer)

- Prestige (The buyer may want the prestige of owning their own business and the stature that may bring in the community)

- Security (The seller and buyer both want to feel that they are making a good, safe deal)

- Fear and Anxiety (These are normal human emotions that factor into every major decision that people make. They are the basis for the "cold feet" syndrome that I discuss in the next chapter)

- Greed (Everyone wants to make the best deal that they can but one of the secrets to successfully buying or selling a business is to negotiate a fair deal for everyone involved)

All of these items are important to consider as you conduct negotiations. Remember, both of you must compromise on some points to close the deal.

The Three-Step Negotiation Process

The best way to conduct negotiations and move to the actual sale of the business should include a three-step process:

1. Execute an Earnest Money Agreement or Letter of Intent (with related Confidentiality Agreement).

2. Accomplish Due Diligence. Obtain and verify all additional necessary information upon which to base an informed buying decision and resolve all points between all parties.

3. Execute a Purchase and Sale Agreement.

In this chapter, I'll talk about these three steps which logically lead to the next chapter where the Closing (the actual sale of the business) will be addressed.

Essential Information Buyers Need

In order for the buyer to effectively evaluate the potential purchase of a business and accomplish the necessary "due diligence," the detailed information regarding the operation of the business needs to be obtained and examined. Chapter 4 contains an extensive discussion of the types of information necessary.

Before I get too far into the negotiation process, it's time to introduce another law of the jungle that's most important for buyers and sellers to be alert to:

Strategic Jungle Law #10:

"Always assume that there are skeletons in the closet!"

This topic is also very important for sellers as it'll give them a guide as to what buyers will be looking for, and what could "kill a deal."

Finding The Skeletons

Most businesses have some negative feature(s) that the sellers will initially not talk about. You can be sure that any problems will come out later as buyers begin analyzing the business, and it could kill the sale if the problems are perceived as a cover-up situation. The reason for this is that buyers will ask themselves (logically) "if they hid this fact from me, what else are they hiding?" Whereas, if the negative aspect(s) is clearly presented and discussed with the buyer, it may not be a serious problem because the buyer may feel that it can be overcome, avoided, or changed. The seller should strongly consider this and determine all of the possible negative factors that could affect the sale of their business. If they're very serious problems the business may not be salable, unless they're corrected first. There are many possible problems with a business and some examples of "skeletons in the closet" include this alphabetized listing:

Accounts Receivable that are uncollectable or extremely past due.

Bad publicity, and/or bad reports at the Better Business Bureau, the Chamber of Commerce, etc.

Credit problems with banks and/or suppliers.

Downward business trends for this particular business.

Expiring patents or licenses federal and/or state law violations that will require a major expense to correct.

Federal and/or state law violations requiring major expense to correct.

Government suspension or revocation of license for regulation violations.

Historic downward business trends in the seller's particular industry.

Increasing difficulty or expense in getting raw materials, products or services.

Jack-of-all-trades owner is the major/only asset. It's a job, not a business.

Key employee(s) leaving or competing with the business.

Litigation, legal claims, encumbrances and liens against the business.

Major new competition being planned (e.g. new shopping center, mega store, etc.)

Non-assignable or non-renewable leases.

Obsolete machinery and/or overvalued inventory.

Product obsolescence.

Quiet! There are no clients, customers or sales revenues.

Rent to be significantly increased (if leased facility).

Seller's personal affairs that may affect the ability to sell the business (e.g., divorce).

Taxes overdue or unpaid (e.g., income, sales, FICA).

Unreported cash revenues that the seller wants considered.

Violations or noncompliance with environmental and/or safety requirements.

Withdrawal of territorial rights from supplier or franchiser.

e**X**tremely large increase in insurance or other required expenses.

Yet another non-performing relative on the payroll or cash-only vendor at the back door.

Zoning violations (e.g., unapproved existing variances) or impending zoning changes.

And lastly the business having any stigma associated with violent crime, drug abuse, pornography, communicable diseases, or similar ills of modern society. This may sound distasteful but a due diligence process should ensure that none of these kinds of problems are impacting the business for sale.

Key Factors In Negotiation

In reality, many people can bring a potential buyer and business seller together. The real challenge is in handling the negotiations between a buyer and seller after the Letter of Intent has been signed. It may seem an academic process now that a buyer has indicated that they want to buy what a seller has to sell. Not so! The majority of business deals that reach the Letter of Intent stage never close! If you understand the various techniques of negotiating a business sale, you'll stand a much better chance of completing the sale. Some of the key factors that will have to be addressed in negotiations include:

- Offering to purchase under certain conditions (Earnest Money Agreement/Letter of Intent)

- Identifying rights to be assigned

- Structuring the business sale

- Negotiating a covenant not to compete

- Negotiating a post-sale consulting contract/employment agreement

- Negotiating seller financing

- Working with attorneys and accountants

- Handling buyer/seller anxiety

- Preparing and executing the Purchase and Sale Agreement

- Preparing counteroffers

- Understanding why some businesses don't sell

I'll discuss each of these areas in the order presented above.

Earnest Money Agreement/ Letter Of Intent

The Letter of Intent is an offer made by a potential buyer to purchase a business under certain conditions. A Letter of Intent states the conditions and time frames within which negotiations will be conducted. A Letter of Intent must contain some amount of Earnest Money (deposit) to signify the buyer's sincerity. Usually, up to 5% of the proposed purchase price is required. This is held in escrow by the business broker or other fiduciary agent. Some of the conditions and contingencies included in the Letter of Intent are:

- Proposed structure of the sale (asset or corporate stock)

- Proposed purchase price

- Proposed payment process (cash, mortgage, promissory note, etc.)

- Rights to be assigned (patents, copyrights, trademarks, trade names, etc.)

- Licenses to be assigned (lottery, liquor, etc.)

- How accounts receivable are to be handled

- Proposed covenant not to compete agreements (previous owner(s) and current seller)

- Proposed apportionment of purchase price (among tangible and intangible assets)

- Verification of business financial statements

- Verification of condition of equipment and fixtures

I've included an example Earnest Money Agreement/Letter of Intent as Appendix C for your reference. Please note that the buyer and seller shouldn't enter into serious negotiation until an Earnest Money Agreement is signed by both parties. This is evidence that there's a broad meeting of the minds, and serious negotiations can begin leading to a Purchase and Sale Agreement and eventually, a closing. It should be noted that although a Letter of Intent has been executed between the buyer and seller, nothing is final until the actual closing and sale of the business.

I've just introduced two concepts in the list above that I've not yet discussed and are important to understand in the negotiation process:

- Rights to be assigned (patents, copyrights, trademarks, trade names)

- Covenant not to compete agreements (previous owner(s) and current seller)

Identifying Rights To Be Assigned

You should know what patents, copyrights, trade names, trademarks, and proprietary information are and the differences between them. They could be crucial to the successful operation of the business, and the seller should disclose to the buyer (and the buyer should make a special effort to find out) just what these are. For your information, I've provided the following brief descriptions for each of these items:

Patents: A patent is a grant of property rights by the U.S. Government through the U.S. Patent and Trademark Office for an invention to an inventor (or their heirs and assignees). The term of the patent is usually for 17 years from the date that the patent is granted. The rights conferred with the patent are, in general, the right to exclude others from making, using, or selling the invention. A patent is a definite commercial advantage if there is a market for the patented product and the rights to the patent may be sold, licensed, and otherwise transferred as part of the business sale. As the buyer, you must make sure that if part (or all) of the basis of the business that you're buying is reliant on patents that the patents are current (how much time is left before the patent expires) and that the patents are transferable (no other claims against the patents).

I once brokered the sale of a manufacturing company whose sole product was a heavy-duty, special-use exercise bicycle used primarily in hospitals and rehabilitation centers. It turned out that the seller of the business had only a license to manufacture the bicycle from the otherwise uninvolved patent owner, and the license wasn't transferable without the approval of the original patent holder. There was approximately five years left on the life of the patent and the manufacturing business was not salable without the patent. The patent holder used this opportunity of the pending business sale to try to increase the royalties from the buyer, and the sale of the business was almost lost. Fortunately, the business sale went through, but not without compromises between the buyer, the seller, and the patent holder. Both buyers and sellers must pay attention to the issue of patents if they're involved in the business.

Copyrights: A copyright is a form of protection provided by the U.S. Government under the Copyright Act to authors of original works of authorship including literary, dramatic, musical, artistic, and certain other intellectual works. Once something is copyrighted, the owner has the following exclusive rights:

- To reproduce the copyrighted work

- To prepare other works based on the copyrighted work

- To distribute copies or recordings of the copyrighted work to the public for sale, rental, lease, or lending

- To perform the copyrighted work publicly in the case of literary, musical, motion pictures or other audio-visual works

- To display the copyrighted work publicly

The types of works of authorship that may qualify for copyright include:

- Literary works (like this book!)

- Musical works (with accompanying words)

- Dramatic works (including accompanying music)

- Pictorial, graphic, and sculptural works

- Motion pictures and other audio-visuals

- Sound recordings

- Architectural works

- Software programs

It's interesting to understand that under the present Copyright Act, copyright protection begins automatically upon the creation of a work, and a work is created when it's fixed in a copy for the first time. In general, copyrights last for 50 years after the death of the author(s), although other conditions apply under varied circumstances.

Under the present law, registration is not a condition of copyright protection, and someone can begin using the copyright symbol © as soon as their work is in document form. However, for maximum protection and ease of enforcement of a copyright, I recommend that all original authored materials be formally registered under the Copyright Act. This is especially important to the buyer of a business to establish the seller as the copyrighted owner of the material to be conveyed as part of the sale and then to purchase the copyright as a specific part of the sale of the business.

Trademarks: A trademark is either a word, phrase, symbol, or design that identifies and distinguishes the source of the goods or services of one party from those of others. A service mark is the same as a trademark except that it identifies and distinguishes the source of a service rather than a product. Trademark rights arise through two different ways:

- Actual use of the mark in interstate commerce

- Registering of the mark in the U.S. Patent and Trademark Office (USPTO)

Unlike copyrights or patents, trademark rights can last indefinitely if the owner continues to use the mark to identify its goods or services. Note that anyone who claims rights to a mark may use the TM (trademark) designation with the mark to alert the public to the claim. However, the claim may or may not be valid. If the trademark has been properly registered at the USPTO, the symbol ® may then be used, and no other entity may legally use the trademark. As a buyer of a business in which a trademark is important, you should determine the status of the trademark (common usage TM or registered ®) and ensure that all rights to the trademark are transferred to the buyer as part of the business sale. It's relatively easy to apply for a trademark if the seller hasn't already done so.

Trade Name: A trade name is either a word, phrase, or name of a person or a combination of words, phrases, or names of people used by manufacturers, industrialists, merchants, and others that identifies and distinguishes one business operation from another. A trade name is much different than a trademark in that there's no federal provision for control and registration of the rights to a trade name. One good test to determine whether something truly qualifies as a trademark rather than a trade name is to look at how the wording is used. Trademarks are always adjectives or adverbs (e.g., BizPricer™ Business Valuation Software), never nouns or verbs. Conversely, trade names are almost always nouns (e.g., Business Book Press is a trade name). Most states require a business when it's incorporated to register a trade name and verify that there's no other business in that state using the same or closely similar name. If the business is operated as a sole proprietorship, there usually is no requirement to file with the Secretary of State and consequently there is no verification of the uniqueness of the trade name within the state. Many (if not all) municipalities require that a business file a form at the city or town hall indicating that they're doing business in that municipality, and this process is commonly referred to as "doing business as" (d/b/a); this establishes some rights to the trade name within that jurisdiction. When you purchase a business, you should ensure that you file the proper paperwork with the state (if applicable) and local municipality to retain your rights in the trade name of the business. As a minimum, always file a "d/b/a", also known as a "fictitious name" at the local town hall.

Proprietary Information: Some businesses have certain information regarding their operation that they consider to be proprietary to themselves. Frequently, this information is written down in working notes and files or may be in the head of the owner or key employees. Be sure to identify the existence of this information and have it transferred in documentation form at the time of the business ownership transfer.

Some examples of proprietary information are:

- Machine setup and jigging processes (primarily manufacturing businesses)

- Recipes (primarily food related businesses)

- Formulas (primarily chemical related businesses)

- Customer lists

- Patterns/specifications

- Operational procedures

- Pricing procedures

- Software (source code) and firmware (these may also be copyrighted or patented)

Structuring The Business Sale

During the negotiation process decisions will have to be made by the buyer and seller about the overall structure of the business sale. The first decision that has to be made is whether the purchase and sale will be an asset sale or a corporate stock sale. I strongly recommend that the sale be structured as an asset sale rather than a corporate stock sale principally for reasons limiting hidden liability that could accrue to the buyer (this was discussed in Chapter 2). Accordingly, this section will primarily address structuring the business sale as an asset sale, but considerations for those buying and/or selling the corporate stock of an incorporated business are also included.

The next step in structuring the business sale after deciding to pursue an asset or stock sale is to identify the assets and agreements that will make up the purchase and sale of the business. Some of the assets that should be included in the purchase and sale include:

- Furniture, fixtures, and equipment

- Inventory (finished goods, work in process, raw material)

- Real estate (land, buildings, leases)

- Trademarks, trade names, patents, copyrights

- Contracts, agreements, licenses, concessions

- Goodwill

At this point in the negotiations, the buyer and seller should have already agreed to a tentative purchase price based on the valuation process described in Chapter 2 (or similar process such as using BizPricer™ Business Valuation Software), and also, what assets that make up the business are to be conveyed at the closing. The primary goal now is to assign portions of the purchase price to the various assets and agreements that are to be conveyed as part of the business sale.

In general, the buyer wants to apportion as much of the purchase price for the business to items that can be expensed rather than to depreciable assets. This provides near-term write-off of those portions of the purchase price. This may not be in conflict with the objectives of the seller because there is very little difference under today's tax code between ordinary income and capital gains.

Whenever possible, independent appraisals of the business's major assets should be obtained. However, a note about real estate appraisals: the buyer should ensure the real estate is appraised at its fair market value for its present use as a site for the business if the business is to remain in that location and the real estate is to be included in the sale. Normally, real estate is appraised at its "highest and best use," unless otherwise specified, which may or may not be the value assigned based on the real estate's current business use. For example, if you're valuing a warehouse facility as the real estate for a wholesale distributorship business that's to be sold as an operating business, the real estate may have less value in its present use than if an appraiser determined that the highest and best use for the land was for a new shopping center. If the buyer had to pay the shopping center land price, it may make the purchase price of the business unworkable. Conversely, the seller should explore the possibility that the real estate may be worth more than the business itself by having a "highest and best use" appraisal done. The seller may want to sell the business as "requiring relocation" if the real estate value is excessive as compared to the business value, and pursue selling the real estate separately.

Now that the general structure of the business sale has been determined (asset or corporate stock, the assets to be conveyed have been identified, and the pertinent appraisals are in hand or have been ordered), the next step in the negotiation process is to identify the various agreements that will be required to be executed between the buyer and seller.

Covenant Not To Compete

There may be an existing Covenant Not To Compete Agreement in place from previous owner(s) of the business for sale, and the buyer will want to ensure that it's transferable. More importantly though, the buyer should insist on a Covenant Not To Compete Agreement with the current seller of the business. It could be a disaster if a buyer purchased a business just to see the seller open an identical or even similar business across the street the next day! There must be an agreement signed by the seller stipulating some reasonable period of time and geographic proximity in which the seller will not conduct the type of business being sold or anything similar. This non-compete agreement is frequently the source of many problems in the negotiation process. The seller usually doesn't want to restrict their options to conduct other business in the future, and the buyer doesn't want to end up in competition with the person who once owned the business. Common sense and logic should prevail here. If the seller isn't willing to agree to a reasonable non-compete agreement that clearly protects the buyer's future interests then the buyer is right to question the seller's motives for the business sale. I've included an example Covenant Not To Compete Agreement as Appendix F for your information.

Seller Consulting Contract

Many business sales include some continuation of involvement by the seller in the ongoing operations of the business after its sale for a specific period of time. I believe that this is crucial to a smooth business transition to a new owner in almost all situations. The business seller almost always has a wealth of knowledge and experience relative to the business operations that can't be transferred in any other way than in direct interaction between the buyer and seller while actually operating the business. I'd consider it a "deal-killer" if the seller wouldn't agree to some form of post-sale consulting or employment contract if the buyer wanted the seller's involvement. Of course, the terms and conditions are open to negotiation and the buyer and seller must be prepared to compromise with each other on this issue. For example, a seller (who perhaps wants to begin retirement) may want as short a period as possible for as much compensation as possible. The buyer on the other hand, will usually want the seller to stay on in the business for a lengthy period at a relatively low compensation level. Some considerations include:

- Consulting contract versus employment agreement

- Time period of agreement

- Compensation level

- Duties and responsibilities

Basically, the difference between a consulting contract and an employment agreement is a tax issue. Under a consulting contract, the buyer pays the seller a fixed amount for a period of time for services rendered. There's no actual payroll entry with the consequent withholding tax, FICA, etc. Under an employment agreement, the buyer pays the seller from the business's payroll as if the seller is an employee. There's essentially no difference to the new owner if there's already a payroll system in place. In some very small businesses where the owner is the only employee, it wouldn't make any sense to set up a payroll system just to pay the seller for a relatively short period of time. Otherwise, it shouldn't matter to the buyer which form the compensation takes and they should agree to whatever method the seller wants.

The time period of the agreement or contract is important to allow enough time for the transfer of key business information to take place. I wouldn't recommend anything less than a full quarter (3 months) except for the smallest most simple business. You may want to structure the agreement around some specific event(s) rather than a set time frame. For example, the buyer may want the seller to introduce the buyer to all major customers, participate in at least one trade show, go through one product line shutdown or changeover, help introduce a new product, participate in at least one buying trip, etc. The buyer and seller together should work out what makes the most sense for the particular type of business involved.

The compensation level for the seller will be a very negotiable item because the buyer should want to allocate as much of the goodwill value in the business purchase price to this item as possible, to allow for immediate deductibility as an expense. The seller generally will want to spread the income from the sale of the business over time (perhaps as an installment sale) and as a minimum may want to spread the compensation for the continued employment over multiple tax years to minimize the personal tax exposure. This is a very good area to move negotiations ahead if they bog down over the price of the business. Many times a buyer will agree to a fairly large compensation agreement with a seller to reduce the overall price of the business that may otherwise get attributed to goodwill and will probably have little ability to be quickly depreciated. The seller generally doesn't care what form the money takes, whether sale of the business assets or post-sale employment income, because the tax treatment is essentially the same (personal income tax rates and capital gains rates are usually 5% apart at most).

The duties and responsibilities for which the seller is being hired can be a touchy area, and it's best if these can be spelled out in writing to the maximum extent possible to avoid disputes after the sale. The buyer should keep in mind that the business has been the seller's primary responsibility for (often) many years, and it might be tough for the seller to emotionally let go. The buyer and seller should try during the negotiation process to provide details as to just what is expected (and perhaps what is not expected) from the seller during the transition period of the employment contract/agreement. The daily schedules and other pertinent related information should also be written down to avoid ill will later.

Financing Considerations

One of the many crucial parts of the purchase or sale of a small business is to establish the financing necessary to accomplish the transaction. This issue is of equal importance to both the buyer and seller of a business. The buyer needs to find the capital necessary to buy the business from the seller under acceptable repayment terms. The seller needs to ensure that the buyer has established a realistic financing arrangement such that they can reasonably expect to receive the agreed upon funds from the buyer. Since many business sales involve some form of seller financing and the seller is likely to be required to take a second security position to any other lender, both parties have a strong interest in the types and conditions of the financing.

There are actually many sources of financing available to the purchaser of a business and frequently the buyer will use not just one of these sources, but a combination of several.

The most frequently used sources of funding are:

- Buyer's personal capital
- Business seller financing
- U.S. Small Business Administration (SBA) Guaranteed Bank Loan
- Commercial bank loan
- Venture capital

By far, the most frequently used funding sources for the purchase of a small business are a combination of a buyer's personal capital and the business seller's financing. However, many transactions are also financed through the SBA's Loan Guarantee program. To a lesser extent, the other sources of funding are also used and they could be an important part of your business purchase financing plan and shouldn't be overlooked for consideration.

As a matter of interest, a study by the Entrepreneurial Research Consortium found that as much as 50% of all small business capitalization needs (including funds for purchasing a business) come from informal financing arrangements such as personal funds and seller financing. This adds up to as much as $20 billion of small business financing!

Buyers should be sure to include a business purchase financing plan as part of their overall business plan. However they do it, a business plan and the related business purchase financing and capitalization plans are absolute musts for the buyer to lay the proper groundwork to move forward with the purchase of an operating business. I'll discuss this further in Chapter 7.

Buyer's Personal Capital

It's usually an absolute must that the buyer will provide some of the capital funds required to purchase a business. Just how much will be a matter of what other type of financing is to be arranged. Almost no source of funding will feel comfortable providing money for the purchase of a business if the buyer isn't providing a significant portion (typically 25% to 50%) of the overall business purchase amount. There are several different categories of this type of funding:

- Personal savings

- Home equity mortgages

- Personal loans from family members

- Personal loans from friends and co-workers

- Loans against paid-up life insurance

Personal Savings

Personal savings are fairly straightforward. It's the discretionary money that the buyer has been able to accumulate to put towards the purchase of their dream; being in business for themselves. However, it's not smart for the buyer to completely allocate all of their available cash to the business purchase. Don't forget to allow for personal and family financial contingencies that may require ready cash. The buyer may also want to explore taking a low interest loan out against a savings account as collateral. Typically, banks will loan up to 90% of a passbook savings account for a relatively low interest rate. This allows the buyer to:

- Maintain an active bank savings account for credit reference purposes

- Continue to receive interest on the savings

- Have a deductible business expense for the interest paid on the "loan" which will substantially reduce its cost

Home Equity Mortgages

Home equity mortgages, also know as second mortgages, are a frequent source of funds for many small business purchasers. This is a relatively inexpensive source of money for the business purchase and a bank can usually be found that won't charge an application fee, appraisal fee, or points. The interest rates vary, but a very attractive rate of 2 to 3 percentage points over the prime rate can usually be found. The Wall Street Journal publishes the current accepted prime rate on a daily basis and many other periodicals such as Money Magazine publish this rate monthly. By the way, Money Magazine also lists the banks that offer the best home equity rates around the country. It may pay to shop around as many big banks will write home equity mortgages outside of their immediate areas.

Typically, a bank will loan from 75% to 85% of the value of a home. If the buyer is like most first time business buyers, they're probably between the ages of 35 and 45 and have owned their own home for 10 to 20 years. Although home values haven't risen in the 1990's like in the past decades, they probably still have a significant amount of equity built up in the home just through the process of paying the mortgage payments every month. Frequently, business buyers can find $25,000 to $50,000 of cash available to them through home equity loans.

One word of advice, however. In general, banks don't really care what someone wants the money for because the loan is protected by a strong asset, but they may get nervous if the buyer makes a point of telling them that they intend to use the money to buy a business and quit their steady paying job. Even if this is the plan, it's best not to advertise this fact during the mortgage application process!

Personal Loans From Family Members

This is probably a very viable source of funds for many would-be business owners. Who knows the buyer better than their own family? Buyers shouldn't hesitate to approach their family members, especially those that are business owners themselves or those who seem to be financially well equipped to invest in a somewhat risky venture. The buyer should always deal with their family in a thoroughly business-like manner. Do all of the normal homework that would normally be done in approaching a commercial lender. The buyer should prepare a realistic business plan and present it to their Uncle Bill with the same professionalism they intend to approach the business. At the time of the loan, the buyer should be sure to execute a formal Promissory Note which spells out all the terms and conditions of the loan. Keep the relationship as professional as possible.

Another source of funds under the category of family is the outright gifts of money from the buyer's parents or anyone else they might expect to inherit from. Under the current IRS rules, anyone can "gift" to anyone else up to $10,000 tax-free in any calendar year. If the buyer fits the typical entrepreneurial business buyer profile of being in the 40ish age range, then typically their parents will be in the 60ish to 70ish age brackets. They may have already decided how they want to distribute their estate and may be more than willing to make early, tax-free distributions to the buyer to help them realize their dream. For example, if both parents are alive and the buyer and spouse need $40,000 of capital to purchase a business, then one parent can gift $10,000 each to the buyer and their spouse, and the other parent can do the same. This is $40,000 of tax-free money the buyer can use in purchasing the business. Of course, many other strategies can be worked out depending on the gift-giver's funds, the buyer's needs, timing, etc. If more money is needed and the gift-givers have the resources, then the example discussed previously could be done on December 31 and repeated a day later on January 1 for a total of $80,000!

Personal Loans From Friends and Co-Workers

Loans to the buyer from friends, co-workers, and other acquaintances are also a potential source of funding for the business purchase, but I recommend that the buyer use this avenue very, very carefully. Friends can easily become enemies over matters of money and it's best to keep friends as friends and not business associates.

Other Personal Loans and Sources of Capital

There are many other areas in a buyer's personal life where they can look to raise some cash to finance the purchase of a business. I'll list a few here to stimulate your thinking.

- Borrow from paid-up whole life insurance policies. The buyer will receive the cash value and still keep the insurance.

- Borrow from 401k and other retirement plans (at this writing, borrowing from a 401k for this purchase is not allowed by the IRS, but there may be ways around this. Check with your CPA).

- Instead of the home equity loans discussed earlier, a buyer many want to refinance the entire first mortgage on their home. They may realize more cash from this and will get a lower interest rate than if they use the second mortgage route.

Business Seller Financing

In most sales of operating businesses, there's some amount of seller financing of the purchase price. This amount can range dramatically depending on circumstances, but frequently falls in the 50% to 75% range of the total purchase price. In most situations, a seller wants to receive as much money "up front" as they can, while a buyer will want to pay out as little as possible. The reasons for this are varied, but basically the seller will need a significant amount of cash to pay the IRS capital gains taxes that will be due upon the sale of the business. The seller will also want to minimize the risk of not receiving the total amount of the business selling price by receiving as much up front as possible. The buyer, on the other hand, will want to minimize their cash outlay to lessen their risk in the business (what if the business isn't as good as represented by the seller?). The buyer will also want to conserve as much ready cash as possible to operate the newly acquired business.

Because this is the predominant form of financing of a small business sale, I'll discuss it further in its own section later in this chapter.

SBA Guaranteed Bank Loans

Many people are misinformed about the SBA's role in the business financing process. In fact, the SBA doesn't loan money directly, but rather guarantees loans to business buyers from commercial banks. However, this is a very powerful guarantee and may make the difference in whether a bank will loan the necessary funds to the buyer. Basically, the SBA will guarantee to the lender the repayment of up to 90% of the amount borrowed. The rules and procedures for applying for SBA guaranteed financing vary from bank to bank. A potential buyer is encouraged to find a convenient commercial bank in their community that participates in the SBA program to learn their particular requirements to process a loan application for the purchase of a small business. In general, the following discussion about Commercial Bank Loans also applies to applications for loans that are SBA guaranteed.

Commercial Bank Loans

Getting financing for the purchase of a business direct from a commercial bank without an SBA guarantee is challenging. For starters, they'll probably want to see a strong financial involvement on the buyer's part and at least some debt financing on the part of the seller. This will show the bank that the buyer and seller both have faith in the continued prosperous operation of the business which will help to alleviate their concerns about being repaid. The more hard assets in the business the better, from the bank's point of view. If the business purchase includes the sale of real estate, this will also work strongly in the borrower's favor. Anything that can be used as a firm collateral base will enhance the buyer's prospects of securing a loan because the bank will know that the debt is reasonably secured by the assets.

In general, banks look at five key factors in deciding whether or not to make a business loan and the buyer should prepare a financing proposal with these factors in mind:

- Is the buyer suited to the business that's being proposed for purchase?

- What specifically will the money be used for in the purchase of the business? To pay the seller? To finance the operational expenses for a period of time? To purchase new equipment? The bank will want to look very closely at the track record for the business being purchased to be satisfied that there's a reasonable likelihood that the business prosperity will continue.

- How will the loan be repaid? A buyer will need to present a strong but realistic statement of future earnings (pro-forma) that the bank will readily believe. Don't forget to include all reasonable expenses that are sometimes overlooked by enthusiastic buyers, including an owner's draw and a reserve for contingency expenses.

- What types of collateral are proposed to be pledged to secure the loan? The stronger the collateral potential, the more likely the bank will be to approve the loan. One of the problems here is that if the seller will also be holding some financing of the purchase price of the business, the bank will insist on being the first mortgage holder against the assets. This will of course relegate the seller to a second mortgage position which may not be acceptable.

- Lastly, the bank will have its loan committee take an overall view of the proposed transaction to satisfy itself that the deal in its totality makes "good business sense." This can be very subjective, but its the bank's money and they certainly have an obligation to minimize their risk to an acceptable level.

If the buyer does get approved for commercial bank financing, they can expect to pay 3 to 5 percentage points over the prime lending rate for a relatively short period of time (5 to 10 years).

Venture Capital

Although using venture capital is an option that the buyer may want to consider in finding the financial wherewithal to purchase a small business, they need to first understand the basic premise of venture capital firms. They essentially exist to provide capital as an investment in an unproven, but extremely high potential business. In general, venture capital companies don't make outright loans. Instead, they buy an equity (ownership) interest in the business. They expect very high potential returns from their investment (five to ten times their investment in as few as five years). Unless the purchaser of a business has an extraordinary idea about how to dramatically increase the business operations and profits, its unlikely that a venture capital firm would shown any interest in funding the purchase of an operating business. If a venture capital firm does get involved in the purchase of the business the seller will most likely find themselves dealing directly with the venture capitalists during negotiations. For further information about venture capital and whether it might be right for your situation, you might try contacting the following resources:

- The National Venture Capital Association (NVCA)
  1655 North Fort Meyer Drive, Suite 850
  Arlington, VA 22209 (Tel: 703-524-2549)
  http://www.nvca.org

- The National Association of Investment Companies
  1300 Pennsylvania Avenue NW Suite 700
  Washington, DC 20004 (Tel: 202-289-4336)

- National Association of Small Business Investment Companies
  666 11th Street NW Suite 750
  Washington, DC 20001 (Tel: 202-628-5055)
  http://www.nasbic.org

- Seed Capital Network
  8905 Kingston Pike Suite 12
  Knoxville, TN 37923
  http://www.seedcapitalnetwork.com

Seller Financing Considerations

The promissory note to the seller from the buyer is a form of deferred compensation from a tax perspective for the seller. As already discussed, in most cases sellers will have to accept a promissory note from the buyer in order to complete the sale. There are several variables that need to be considered from both perspectives:

- Amount of the promissory note

- Interest rate and period over which it is to be paid

- Security for the promissory note

The principal amount of the promissory note (the amount of money owed) is usually not as flexible and able to be changed as is the interest rate and period of time over which payments are to be made. If the business has been fairly valued, there should be enough cash flow from business operations to cover the payments the buyer must make to the seller. Remember, the business must be able to pay itself off through cash flow over a reasonable length of time. The seller will want to ensure that the amount of the note doesn't exceed the fair market value of the assets in the business that are being used as security for the note (more about security later). Sometimes a buyer will need to provide more cash down (20% to 50% of the purchase price is customary) to lower the amount of money owed, and therefore lower the amount of the payments.

The interest rate and time period of the note are key factors in determining whether the business can afford to pay for itself. Interest rates charged by the seller are usually pegged to the prevailing best bank loan rates or somewhat lower. The seller has to be careful about setting the interest rate too far below bank rates because the IRS has the ability to "impute" a fair market interest rate if they determine that the interest rate is too low. Impute means that they'll tax a seller as if the rate was 8% rather than, say, the 4% rate actually being charged. However, there's usually a wide latitude for negotiation here as the best bank rate (prime rate) is about 7% at the time of this writing, and many commercial loans are being written at rates up to 12%. To give you an idea of the difference that the spread of interest rates can make in the amount of a $435,400 note (remember our XYZ Company?) amortized over ten years, consider the following:

$435,400 for 10 years @ 4% is $4,408 monthly

$435,400 for 10 years @ 7% is $5,055 monthly

$435,400 for 10 years @ 10% is $5,754 monthly

$435,400 for 10 years @ 12% is $6,247 monthly

The time period of the note is also a key factor when considering the financing of a business sale. The seller and buyer will both usually want the note paid off as soon as possible for different reasons. The seller will want to collect the money for the business to "cash out" as soon as possible to minimize the risk that the money won't be paid. The seller's biggest fear in accepting a note for the business is that the buyer will run the business into the ground, effectively making the business assets worthless, and then won't pay the Promissory Note. The seller would then recover a business with little or no value and have received only a portion of the business's original value. The buyer wants to pay off the note as soon as possible within the constraints of the business's cash flow so that the maximum financial benefits can be realized. For these reasons, most business sale promissory notes have a time frame in the 5 to 10 year range. To see the effect that the different time frames have on payments at a particular interest rate, the following calculations are offered. I've picked 10% as a representative interest rate for illustration purposes:

$435,400 @ 10% for 10 years is $ 5,754 monthly

$435,400 @ 10% for 8 years is $ 6,607 monthly

$435,400 @ 10% for 6 years is $ 8,066 monthly

$435,400 @ 10% for 4 years is $11,043 monthly

Obviously, from the data presented above, the interest rate and time frame of a Promissory Note can have widely different effects on the business's ability to pay the note off. Herein lies fertile ground for negotiations between the buyer and seller.

Security for the Promissory Note from the buyer to the seller can be a very sticky wicket. The buyer normally wants to secure the Note with the business assets (after all, didn't the buyer and seller just agree as to what the business is worth?); and the seller normally wants to secure the Note with the personal assets of the buyer (because the buyer could run the business into the ground and leave no assets for the seller to recover in the event of a default). This is a dilemma! The problem here is that both the buyer and seller are right to some extent, which in itself suggests the solution. The best approach here is for a 50-50 compromise between the buyer and seller. Half the note amount should be secured by the buyer's personal assets and half should be secured by the business assets. This results in the buyer assuming somewhat more risk than the seller due to the cash that the buyer has already provided as part of the purchase. This is generally seen as fair by the buyers because they control the business assets, and therefore, logically should accept greater risk. This doesn't always work out quite so neatly, so the buyer and seller should address this issue early in negotiations to make sure that it won't be a deal killer.

Working With the Deal Killers

Professional advisors to both the seller and buyer in the purchase and sale of a business are extremely important; but I want to stress the word advisor. One of the keys to successfully negotiating a business purchase and sale is for the buyer and seller to have extensive face to face negotiations on the major points of the proposed sale without having the respective attorneys and accountants involved in that part of the process. I discussed in Chapter 1 the problems that most buyers and sellers have with attorneys that represent them. The attorneys frequently see their role as trying to get the best deal for their clients. If both the seller's and buyer's attorneys take this position, there will be no sale of the business because usually there can't be two best deals (win-win concepts notwithstanding). What the buyer and seller need to strive for and to communicate to their advisors is that they want a fair deal and they want to complete the deal, if at all possible. Before involving professional advisors in the purchase and sale of a business, the buyer and seller may want to have:

- A general agreement that the buyer wants to buy and the seller wants to sell the business

- A broad outline of what's being sold and whether this is to be an asset or corporate stock sale (this should include a description of the business and its parts that are to be transferred)

- A tentative selling/purchase price for the business (both the seller and buyer may want to involve their accountants in the business valuation process)

- An understanding of the key terms and conditions of the sale to include such things as time frames, seller financing, seller covenants, warranties, and employment agreements

The seller and buyer may want to include the business broker (if one is involved) in these early discussions to help them reach some common ground on the major issues and to suggest the items that should be discussed and agreed to. In fact, I strongly recommend that the business broker be involved, but the buyer should never forget who the broker works for. When the buyer and seller have a general meeting of the minds, this is the time for an Earnest Money Agreement /Letter of Intent to be executed between them to allow the process of the sale to move forward. It's at this time that it's most important to involve the respective attorneys to review the Letter of Intent that's to be signed and to begin work on the details of the Purchase and Sale Agreement that will form the structure of the actual purchase.

Handling Buyer/Seller Anxiety

There will be many reasons and sources of both buyer and seller anxiety as the negotiations continue. The buyer, seller, and broker should all be prepared for this and understand that the purchase and sale of a business is a major financially significant event in the lives of both parties. Additionally, the buyer and seller will be making emotional as well as business commitments that will lead to nervousness and second-guessing. It's important for everyone involved to recognize the potential for this to happen and to carefully and methodically deal with each problem as it arises.

The following discussion addresses a few specific things that have worked to help alleviate buyer and seller anxiety.

If a buyer is concerned that the seller won't comply with certain agreements to be completed after the sale, such as an employment contract, the concern may be alleviated by requiring a certain amount of the cash in the transaction to be held in escrow by a neutral third party. The funds will only be disbursed upon compliance with the agreement as determined by the third party.

Sometimes during the negotiation process a seller begins to believe the sales hyperbole and the very rosy picture being painted by themselves and the broker. It's normal that someone selling something tends to exaggerate its good features and minimize any negative features, and this is also true in the process of selling a business. Sellers, as operators of small businesses are usually very good salespersons/marketers, and they must guard against "selling themselves" as they and their brokers present the business in its best light. Sellers must be realistic and keep in mind the reasons that motivated them to begin the selling process in the first place. Those reasons were most likely evolved over a long period of time and based on some sound fundamental reasons (retirement, health, etc.) and the optimistic projections being presented to a buyer may be true, but they shouldn't change the fundamental decision on the part of the seller to sell the business.

It's usually better to have a few long "grind it out" negotiation sessions than it is to have many short meetings and telephone calls. During longer meetings, the many interconnected issues can be discussed together rather than piecemeal, and many problems that are relative to each other can be worked out on the spot. This will move the negotiation process ahead faster and will minimize the opportunity for confusion about small, but important issues. The other advantage with fewer, longer negotiation sessions is that it allows for planning and participation by all of the principals involved; the buyer, the seller, the advisors, and the broker all can plan to be together with the needed information. This alone will solve many of the anxiety problems that arise in the negotiation process.

If negotiations start to bog down over a particular point, the buyer and seller should temporarily set aside the tough issues and work on easier issues to resolve. The process of making progress, even if it's relatively small, will lessen anxiety and help to build trust between the buyer and seller and may establish a basis for agreement on the tougher issues. Another good negotiation technique related to this is for the buyer and seller to begin to trade negotiation issues with each other. For example: "I'll agree to a higher inventory valuation if you'll agree to a longer Promissory Note period." There are many points that buyers and sellers can trade off with each other that will keep the negotiation process moving forward to a successful closing.

Some other areas that buyers and sellers may want to keep in mind in an attempt to minimize anxiety:

- Bring advisors into the negotiations only at key points

- Never let yourself get emotional; it usually overrules common sense

- Work to develop mutual trust by full disclosure of facts and "giving in" in areas that the other doesn't expect

- Keep your eye on the big picture of the purchase and sale of the business with the result being a fair deal for all concerned

Counteroffers

Unless the buyer has offered to buy the business for the exact price and under the exact terms as the seller wants, there will be no closing unless someone modifies their position. The trick is for the seller and buyer to reach a meeting of the minds.

If you're the seller (or the seller's representative) and a lower or otherwise substantially different offer is made for a business, you must insist on understanding why the potential buyer is making that particular offer. Is it because the expenses have been restructured more conservatively than from the seller's point of view? Is it because the buyer's debt service will be higher than the seller anticipated? Is it because the buyer believes the business sales will suffer at first without the seller being available? Is it because the buyer expects a higher ROI than the seller has estimated? Or, is it just because the buyer is bottom fishing and has low-balled the deal? The seller must know the basis of the offer to deal intelligently with the buyer and discuss the pros and cons of the situation. Motivated sellers always develop a counteroffer; one that they feel the buyer can live with based on the buyer's particular financial ability and their analysis of the business.

Some counteroffer possibilities that can be considered are:

a) A given offering price at specific terms can be increased by lengthening the term and/or decreasing the interest rate if the seller has agreed to a payout. For example, using the XYZ Company:

$435,400 at 12% for 10 years = $6,247/month

$493,149 at 9% for 10 years = $6,247/month

$548,931 at 9% for 12 years = $6,247/month

In this particular example, you can see that the offering price for a business can be increased by $57,749 ($493,149 – $435,400) by decreasing the interest rate from 12% to 9%. Also, the offering price can be increased by $113,531 ($548,931 – $435,400) by decreasing the interest rate from 12% to 9% and increasing the term from 10 to 12 years. In these three cases, the monthly payments by the buyer have stayed the same. The buyer certainly can't claim that the cash flow projections wouldn't support the higher price.

b) If the seller hasn't agreed to a payout and there's a shortfall between the buyer's cash down payment and the available financing, the seller may take a Promissory Note for the balance.

c) Other ways of dealing with the costs associated with a Promissory Note are to put in special provisions for balloon payments and/or deferred principal payments. Under a balloon payment and/or a deferred principal payment schedule, the buyer would pay a reduced amount for a period of time, then have the total remaining principal due and payable in full. This strategy may be used to allow a buyer to build up a track record and a credit history in a business and then secure bank financing at a later date. For example, a seller may balk at agreeing to a 10-year Promissory Note, but will accept a 5-year Note. The problem is that there may not be enough cash flow in the business to support a 5-year payout. Here's what can be done:

- The seller and buyer agree to a Promissory Note that requires monthly payments on a 10-year amortization schedule, but requires a balloon payment of the remaining principal amount due at the end of the fifth year. The premise is that the business can afford the monthly payments under the 10-year schedule and at the fifth year, the new business owner will be able to secure bank financing (or other financing) to pay off the seller in full and have a new bank Note amortization schedule that the business will be able to handle.

Let's look at some numbers to illustrate this point. Let's say that the amount that needs to be financed is $435,400. The seller and buyer both agree to an interest rate of 12%, but the seller wants the money in 5 years and the monthly cash flow from the business operations available for financing the business purchase is projected to be about $6,247 (sound familiar?):

$435,400 @ 12% for 10 years = $6,247 monthly

$435,400 @ 12% for 5 years = $9,685 monthly

Clearly, the business cash flow won't allow a 5-year period for the Promissory Note. However, if the buyer agrees to a balloon payment for the principal remaining at the end of 5 years, the amount will be approximately $280,835. The new business owner can then finance this balance through a conventional lending institution (assuming the business has continued to operate profitably and a good credit record has been developed) under the following terms (keeping the monthly payment constant at $6,247):

$280,835 @ 12% with monthly payments of $6,247 = 5 years

Of course, there may be other costs associated with receiving the bank loan (appraisal fees, credit checks, and mortgage points), but these may be acceptable to the buyer as a way of making the deal work. Actually, the monthly payments could actually go down if the interest rate could be lowered and/or the time period extended beyond 5 years.

Clearly, there's an almost infinite variety of possibilities that could be considered for the many different business negotiation situations that could arise. These examples here are to give the buyer and seller food for thought about how to get together on a financial basis when they're seemingly very far apart on the purchase price.

The Purchase And Sale Agreement

The Purchase and Sale Agreement is really the blueprint for the actual sale of the business from which all parties (the buyer, the seller, the respective attorneys, accountants, and broker), will take specific actions within or by specified times to bring the business sale to a closing. The Purchase and Sale Agreement is a result of the negotiation process that started with the Earnest Money Agreement and should be a recital of everything that was agreed to between the buyer and seller. The following is a checklist for items to be included in a Purchase and Sale Agreement. Note that even if the buyer is only buying the business assets from a seller and not corporate stock, many of the items referring to a corporation will be required if the business being sold is incorporated.

❑ *Identification of buyer(s) and seller(s)*
- Names
- Addresses
- State of incorporation (if incorporated)
- Partnership (if applicable)
- Sole proprietorship trade name (if applicable)

❑ *Characterization of transaction*
- Asset sale
- Corporate stock sale

❑ *Recitals*
- Description of business
- Desire of seller(s) to sell and buyer(s) to buy
- Authorized stock of seller or buyer or both (if incorporated)
- Approval of transaction by directors (if incorporated)
- Approval of transaction by shareholders (if incorporated)
- Approval of transaction by partner(s) (if partnership)

❑ *Assets subject to agreement*
- Securities
- Real estate
- Furniture, fixtures, and equipment
- Patents, copyrights, trademarks, trade names
- Goodwill
- Other assets

❑ *Amount of consideration*
- Single sum
- Aggregate of sums allocated to various assets
- Nature of consideration
- Cash – stock
- Assumption of debts and liabilities
- Other consideration

❑ *Time and manner of payment*
- Transfer of cash, stock, and other consideration at closing
- Installment payments (Promissory Note, if applicable)
- Security for payments

❑ *Conditions precedent to obligations of buyer(s) and seller(s)*
- Consent of shareholders/directors/partners
- Securities registration (if buying stock)
- Approval by lawyers, accountants, or both
- Other requisite approvals
- Compliance with terms of Agreement

❑ *Receipts for clearance of contributions and payments by seller*
- Taxes
- FICA
- Others

❑ *Assumption of employee benefit plans and stock options*

❑ *Covenant against declaration of dividends or changes in stock ownership (if a stock sale)*

❑ *Closing*
- Payment of consideration
- Delivery of instruments of transfer
- Delivery of certificates required by statute (law)
- Acquisition of necessary approvals and rulings
- Adjustments in purchase price at closing
- Conduct of business until closing
- Date of closing

❑ *Inspection of books, records, and premises*

❑ *Representations and warranties by seller*
- Corporate (or otherwise) ownership of assets
- Corporation validly organized and in good standing

- Authorization of sale by directors and shareholders
- Accuracy and completeness of financial statements
- All outstanding liens, contracts, and other obligations disclosed or extinguished
- Absence of subsidiaries
- Absence of labor grievances or actions
- Validity of patents, copyrights, trademarks, and trade names
- Care and preservation of property and assets
- Compliance with all laws affecting business

❏ *Indemnification of buyer(s) by seller(s)*
- Against liabilities not expressly assumed
- Against damages resulting from breach of warranty

❏ *Representations by buyer*
- Corporation validly organized and in good standing (if buyer is incorporated)
- Capital structure; validity of stock to be used in acquisition (if applicable)
- Authorization of acquisition by directors, shareholders, partners (if applicable)

❏ *Assumption by buyer of all or specified liabilities*

❏ *Assumption by buyer of seller's collective bargaining agreement*

❏ *Payment of business broker's commission*

❏ *Compliance with UCC Article 6 and other bulk transfer issues*

❏ *Covenant Not To Compete by seller(s)*

❏ *License to buyer to use seller's trade name*

❏ *Employment of seller's personnel by buyer*

❏ *Resignation of seller's directors and officers (if applicable)*

❏ *Retention of stock by seller as security (if applicable)*

❏ *Risk of loss*

❏ *Assignability of rights under Purchase and Sale Agreement*

❏ *Modification of Purchase and Sale Agreement*

❏ *Remedies for default by buyer or seller*

❏ *Arbitration or mediation of disputes*

❏ *Manner of giving notice*

❏ *Binding of Purchase and Sale Agreement on successor & assigns*

❏ *Governing law applicability*

❏ *Date of execution*

❏ *Signatures*

❏ *Corporate seal(s) (if applicable)*

❏ *Acknowledgments*

I have included an example Purchase and Sale Agreement as Appendix G.

Why Some Businesses Don't Sell

As the last section in this chapter, I've decided to include a description of some of the many reasons that some businesses don't sell. You should use this information relative to your own conduct of negotiations to avoid these pitfalls experienced by others. Earlier I told you that only 20% to 25% of all businesses put "on the market" for sale actually sell (at least at their initial offering). Another way of looking at this is that 75% to 80% of all businesses for sale don't sell for one reason or another. It's probably useful for both buyers and sellers to review some of the reasons I've observed about why deals never actually close. Maybe forewarned is forearmed! Anyway, I've broken down the blame for the failure for a business to close to basically four reasons:

1. The seller's fault

2. The buyer's fault

3. The advisor's fault (*remember Jungle Law #1, "lawyers are deal killers"*)

4. Things just happen

Let's cover each one in order:

The Seller

a) The seller of the business may not be a truly motivated seller. There may be no special reason for selling and in a moment of frustration with a temporary problem, the seller says "I'm out of here" and lists the business for sale with a broker or puts an ad in the paper. When the problem goes away in time, the seller regrets putting the business up for sale and then refuses to adequately cooperate with the broker and any potential buyers that come along. A good broker or careful buyer should be able to spot this problem seller early on. A lack of cooperation on the part of the seller in supplying crucial information to the buyer is a sure tip-off that you're dealing with a reluctant seller.

b) The seller of the business may only be test marketing the business to see if it's actually salable and for what price. These sellers are dishonest with everyone involved in that they waste everyone's time; but again, you should be able to spot these sellers early on. If a seller won't supply you with crucial financial data supported by Federal IRS Tax Returns, even after the buyer has signed a Confidentiality Agreement, then it's a reasonably good assumption that the seller isn't serious.

c) Some sellers have no intention of ever selling the business to a third party and are just using the broker and the selling process to establish a fair market price for their business so that they can transfer ownership to a child, relative, or other closely associated person. These sellers are too greedy to pay a professional for an appraisal of their business and see the sham selling process as a way to get a free valuation from a business broker. Let me tell you, I've been burned by these sellers more than once! The way I've learned to deal with this situation as a business broker is to charge an up front fee for a business valuation before I take the listing. I may lose a few very good business sellers this way, but it works out in the long run in that I weed out the non-serious seller, whatever their reason. For you buyers, the best tip-off that a seller may not be serious for this reason or something similar is if the asking price for the business is exorbitantly high relative to the valuation process that I've described in Chapter 2. In addition, the seller may refuse to negotiate in good faith to a more reasonable position. A buyer should ask a listing broker if an up front fee for a business valuation has been paid. This may give you some insight into how serious the seller is in selling.

d) Some (actually, many) sellers have an unrealistic idea of what their business is really worth. Many sellers fail to take into consideration the need for the buyer to be able to finance the business sale out of the cash flow of the business and they also usually overlook the need for the buyer to pay income tax on the business profits (even though they themselves pay taxes). By far, business sellers putting an unrealistically high price on their business and their reluctance to negotiate a fair price are the biggest reasons that some businesses simply don't sell.

e) Some sellers don't disclose to the buyer early on in the negotiation process all those "skeletons in the closet" that were discussed earlier in this chapter. Most problems can be resolved if they're disclosed openly and honestly and a potential buyer is allowed to develop new approaches on how to deal with the issue(s). Many potential buyers bring a fresh outlook and new ideas to a business situation and surprisingly they're able to come up with ways to resolve problems if they know about them well in advance of the closing. When problems are discovered at the last minute by the buyer, trust may be irretrievably lost, and the deal will never close.

f) Some sellers never bother to check out all of the personal ramifications of the sale of the business such as tax consequences. It always amazes me when sellers discover for the first time that they actually have to pay income tax on the sale of the business and that they then won't have anywhere near the cash in their pocket that they expected. It's always prudent to ask sellers if they have fully consulted with a lawyer and tax accountant about the legal and tax ramifications of selling their business.

g) A seller may just get cold feet about selling the business that has been a lifetime involvement. Emotion plays a very important role in selling a business and many otherwise well-structured business sales haven't closed because the seller just couldn't go through with the sale.

The Buyer

a) There are many, many potential buyers out there that will never buy a business because they lack the true motivation to proceed with this complicated and risky transaction. For many people, it's the American dream to be in business for yourself (no bosses, layoffs, timecards, etc.). When they truly get immersed in the actual purchase process and realize just how hard things are and they're trading one master for another, they head for the hills. For first-time business buyers, the seller should find out what knowledge they actually have about running a business. Truly motivated buyers will already have taken courses from the SBA or the local university that provide training in the running of a small business. Sellers and brokers must qualify their buyer regarding motivation and ability or everyone's time will be wasted because the unmotivated, incapable buyer will never proceed with the closing.

b) Many buyers just don't have enough money (or access to money) to complete the transaction. It's very expensive to buy even the most modest of businesses when you consider the cash down, the operating capital required, and the myriad of legal and accounting fees encumbered relative to the transaction. Sellers and brokers should understand that no matter how good a sales job they do on an otherwise motivated buyer, if they don't have the money to buy the business, then everyone's time is wasted. A buyer must be financially qualified.

c) Another major obstacle presented by a buyer in purchasing a business is a disagreement over the price. Just as the seller often wants too high a price for the business, the buyer frequently wants to pay too little. If both parties use my recommended capitalization of net profit approach to valuation, this problem should be overcome.

The Advisors

The advisors to both the seller and the buyer are frequently the major cause of a business not being sold. Remember the law of the jungle that lawyers are deal killers and you can sometimes put accountants in this category too. The major problem here is that the advisors too often see themselves in the role of getting the best deal for their clients instead of a fair deal. If both sides are trying to get the best deal, the deal will never happen as there usually isn't two best deals in the same transaction. The lawyers and accountants have to be told by the buyer and seller that they want to do this deal and that they want solutions to issues, not strategies to get the best of the other party.

Things Just Happen

a) I once represented a very successful major landmark restaurant for sale and found two partners with strong food industry experience who were truly motivated to buy and had the financial backing from a venture capital group who believed in them. I carefully prepared an Earnest Money Agreement/Letter of Intent close to the asking price of the business (I had done the valuation and had the business priced fairly). I'd included much of the detail that would normally go into a Purchase and Sale Agreement. The sellers were also truly motivated as they were in their 70's and planning to retire to Greece after the business sale. I was almost counting my commission! On the day that I and the buyers were to present the Letter of Intent (with a check for $25,000), we arrived at the restaurant at the agreed upon time (on a Monday when it was normally closed) only to find that a major fire had occurred the night before and destroyed the building structure. I'm not one to be easily daunted by things, so I still tried to present the Letter of Intent only to find out that the sellers were self-insured relative to the real estate and they now insisted on adding $150,000 to the selling price of the business to cover the cost of repairs. Needless to say, the deal fell through, and my buyers went elsewhere to a more reasonably priced situation. Like I said, things just happen.

b) Other situations that may occur that fall under this category include:

• The landlord won't assign the necessary lease to continue the business operation or demands an exorbitant increase in rent

- An unexpected IRS audit during the negotiation process turns up "irregularities" in the business's bookkeeping

- A buyer or seller dies or otherwise becomes physically unable to proceed with the transaction

- Previously unknown creditors to the business pop up at the last minute

- Unknown environmental violations surface that are expensive to rectify (asbestos, lead paint, leaking fuel storage tanks, radon, etc.)

- It turns out that the seller doesn't really own the patent that they thought they had purchased; they only bought the non-assignable rights to it

- A long ago partner or family member shows up just before closing to try to claim "their share" of the proceeds from the seller

- Some stockholders object to the sale

Additional Considerations For A Franchise

It's especially important to check all of the details in franchise agreements if the business being purchased includes a franchise. I first discussed this issue in Chapter 3 and I want to highlight the point here as a way of illustrating negotiation procedures by using a personal anecdote:

A retail franchised business operation was about to go to closing when the buyer was told by the franchiser that an escrow of $50,000 was needed to cover mandatory site upgrades in accordance with the Franchise Agreement. Sure enough, buried deep within the agreement on page 23 was a stipulation that every ten years the franchiser had the option of requiring the franchisee to remodel and upgrade the physical condition of the business site. The ten year period was about up and the alterations required were estimated to cost approximately $50,000! This just about killed the deal, but it was saved by those involved in the following way:

- The franchiser agreed to extend the deadline for the upgrade by two years.

- The franchiser agreed to take only half of the required escrow amount in monthly payments (added to the royalty fees) for the next two years.

• The seller agreed to extend the buyer's Promissory Note payment period out enough time (approximately two years) to reduce the monthly costs to the buyer just enough to offset the increased cash flow requirements for the real estate upgrade.

The business deal closed with the franchiser satisfied that the renovations would ultimately take place, the seller was happy because the selling price remained the same (although the payoff period was a little longer), the buyer was happy about getting the business they wanted with no increase in the cash flow in the crucial first two years, the broker was happy about receiving the commission, and of course the lawyers were happy because they receive their fee either way!

7

Closing The Deal

- *The Buyer's Responsibilities*
- *The Seller's Responsibilities*
- *The Business Broker's Responsibilities*
- *Closing Checklist*

Closing the deal is the hardest to accomplish, but usually the shortest part of buying or selling an operating business. After all, the valuations, investigations, and negotiations are complete and now it's a matter of getting everything into writing in a form that satisfies everyone so that the transfer of ownership of the business can take place. However, you can definitely count on the following law of the jungle to take place:

Strategic Jungle Law #11:

"Someone will always get cold feet just before the closing!"

Be prepared for this! The seller and buyer may both start to wonder if they're really getting a fair deal. The best way to get ready for this is to anticipate it happening and then to deal logically and reasonably with it at the time. The best situation for all parties is to follow an orderly buying and selling process that will move things along in a business-like manner. The major elements of the business purchase and sale process are:

- Earnest Money Agreement/Letter of Intent (previously discussed)

- Purchase and Sale Agreement (previously discussed)

- Closing (at which actual title and ownership of the business is conveyed)

This chapter will deal primarily with identifying everyone's responsibilities after the Purchase and Sale Agreement has been executed and closing the deal at a formal Closing. At this Closing, the actual legal instruments of transfer are signed, money and/or promissory notes are exchanged, and the buyer becomes the new owner of the business. The Closing date and place are set to everyone's convenience and all of the pre-closing tasks are assigned to the various parties for completion.

Now that the Purchase and Sale Agreement has been signed by both the seller and buyer, there's an excellent chance that the sale will actually take place. But there's another important law of the jungle that occurs at this point that must be understood and dealt with or the purchase and sale of the business will never be completed:

Strategic Jungle Law #12:

"Negotiations must stop at the signing of the Purchase and Sale Agreement!"

There must be an end to the negotiation process or things will begin to unravel. The deal at this point is like a house of cards with many parts of the negotiated deal contingent on another part. Trying to reopen negotiations after a Purchase and Sale Agreement has been signed will most likely lead to a collapse of the entire deal as one thing affects another, and everyone begins to lose patience.

However, this is no time for anyone to sit back as if the deal was done! All parties have worked very hard to get the business sale to this point and a little more work on everyone's part will help to see the deal through. The following discussion concerns the responsibilities of the various parties, and the business brokers should make it their responsibility to see that everyone else follows through on theirs.

The Buyer's Responsibilities

The buyer's and/or the business's attorney's responsibilities will include:

- Finalizing financial arrangements

- Reviewing/signing any necessary leases

- Applying for licenses and permits

- Complying with the Bulk Sales Law

- Preparing any additional legal documentation required by the Purchase and Sale Agreement

- Taking inventory of finished goods and work in process

- Final inspection of the business assets

Each of these responsibilities is explained in more detail below.

Financing Arrangements: The buyer should be completing the financing arrangements with the bank, a mortgage company, the seller (Promissory Note), or whatever other sources have been identified. The buyer should have contingency plans ready if one financing source doesn't come through. Identify another bank or mortgage lender that you can go to right away if the first source doesn't come through.

Review and Sign Lease: The buyer should review and sign the real estate lease as soon as possible. If there are any unforeseen snags, they must be resolved immediately. The buyer should know when a problem develops and be ready to suggest a possible compromise to the other parties involved.

Apply for Licenses and/or Permits: The buyer should apply immediately for all licenses and permits that are needed to operate the business. There's always red tape involved in this bureaucratic process and it could hold up the business sale if not handled as quickly as possible.

Complying With The Bulk Sales Law: The buyer must comply with the state's Bulk Sales Law by notifying the business creditors of the impending sale (minimum time before sale varies by state). This procedure is for the buyer's protection as well as the creditors, but doesn't apply to all businesses. Usually service (no inventory) type businesses are exempt. The broker and the buyer should discuss this and ensure that proper notification is made to the business creditors when the creditor list is received from the seller. This is described further under the seller's responsibilities in the next section.

Preparation of Legal Documentation: The buyer may be required by the Purchase and Sale Agreement to prepare certain legal documentation necessary for the closing. For example: real estate deed, security requirements, seller work contracts, covenants (e.g., not to compete). The buyer should be aware of what these are and make sure the buyer's attorney is actually preparing them.

Taking Inventory: The buyer will most likely want to take an actual physical inventory of the business goods and assets just prior to the closing. The buyer will also want to make a final inspection of the business to ensure that everything is in order. The buyer should plan for enough people to actually take the inventory in the allotted time.

Final Inspection of the Business Assets: The buyer should make a final inspection of the business assets to be conveyed to verify the condition, quantity, status, etc., just before the closing takes place.

The Seller's Responsibilities

The seller's and/or seller's attorney's responsibilities will include:

- Preparing the real estate lease

- Preparing the Promissory Note

- Complying with the Bulk Sales Law

- Settling all liabilities and liens

- Providing for an inspection of the business and an inventory count by buyer

- Preparing any additional legal documentation required

- Complying with any other provisions in the Purchase and Sale Agreement

The seller's responsibilities as identified above are discussed in more detail below.

Prepare Lease for Real Estate: If a lease of real estate is involved from the seller, it must be prepared and presented to the buyer for review and signature. This must be done as soon as possible. Many times problems develop as the result of lease wording and enough time needs to be allowed for these problems to be resolved.

Prepare Promissory Note: Frequently, the seller will prepare the Promissory Note for the buyer under an installment sale or payout. The business broker should make sure that whoever is responsible, they are aware of it and are indeed preparing the note.

Ensure Compliance with Bulk Sales Law: The Bulk Sales Law must be complied with by the seller in that the seller must supply a list (Affidavit) of all the business creditors and debt level. The Affidavit is then signed and presented to the buyer. The buyer (as discussed previously) will notify all of the creditors against a secret sale of the business assets that they may have a claim to and to protect the buyer against hidden or unforeseen business liabilities. The business broker should see that the seller prepares the Affidavit in a timely manner and delivers it to the buyer.

Settling Liabilities and/or Liens: The seller must settle or make appropriate arrangements for otherwise handling the liabilities and/or liens against the business that haven't been agreed to be assumed by the buyer as part of the sale. If a seller tries to push previously unknown liabilities onto a buyer at the Closing, a successful sale may be in jeopardy. The business broker may want to get involved in this aspect of the seller's responsibilities to ensure that this happens.

Facilitate Inspection and Inventory: The seller must make arrangements for the buyer to take a full inventory of all business assets just prior to the Closing. Usually this occurs on the day of the Closing or the day before. The seller should have all of the inventory invoices available to verify the cost of inventory, if necessary.

Prepare Requisite Closing Documentation: The seller may be required by the Purchase and Sale Agreement to prepare certain legal documentation necessary for the Closing. These may include title transfers, bills of sale, competition covenants, and security filings. The seller should be aware of what these are and make sure that the seller's attorney is actually preparing them.

The Business Broker's Responsibilities

The business broker's responsibilities will include:

- Ensuring buyer/seller responsibilities are carried out

- Arranging for third-party leases

- Acting as a go-between

- Handling buyer/seller anxiety

- Participating in the closing

Oversee Buyer and Seller Responsibilities: The most important responsibility of the business broker is to ensure the responsibilities of the seller and buyer are carried out by them in a timely manner. The business broker should ensure that they obtain a copy of the Purchase and Sale Agreement and prepare a list of the seller's and buyer's responsibilities for the Closing. The broker should be in frequent contact with both the seller and buyer and use a list of buyer and seller responsibilities as a check-off as they complete each of their requirements. Whenever a snag develops, the business broker should immediately offer to help in whatever way possible. Someone must keep the ball rolling!

Arrange Third Party Leases: If a lease is required from a third party, it should be the responsibility of the business broker to see that it's prepared and delivered to the buyer. The business broker should do this as soon as possible so there will be time available to resolve disagreements. The business broker should be prepared to negotiate between the landlord and the buyer, if necessary. This responsibility should not be taken lightly because a significant number of closings fall apart as the result of the inability of a prospective buyer to obtain a satisfactory lease of the business premises.

Role as Go-Between: The business broker should act as the go-between in any disagreement or question that may arise between buyer and seller. The business broker should not forget that as the most "neutral" party in this transaction an important role in resolving buyer-seller disputes can be played. Business brokers should make it their job to see that all document transfers are accomplished as quickly as possible.

Handling/Resolving Buyer and Seller Anxieties: Just as was discussed in the previous chapter concerning negotiations, the business broker will have to learn to identify and resolve "cold feet" problems on the part of the seller and buyer. If the business broker notices a definite lack of cooperation from either party, then the broker should get that person into the office as soon as possible. Discuss with the person their previously stated reasons for selling/buying, and point out that those reasons are still valid. The business broker may have to handle this situation very subtly, and it's best to ease into it on a very friendly basis. At all costs, the business broker must avoid alienating the buyer and seller and must rebuild their confidence in their earlier decision to buy/sell the business.

Participation in the Closing: The business broker usually participates at the Closing, if for no other reason than to collect the commission. However, the business broker should be there to help arbitrate any last minute disputes that may arise and to write a check from the Brokerage's trust account for the amount of the escrowed funds. Another factor that must be considered, no matter how unpleasant, involves "shorting the broker." This situation arises from two possibilities: seller's greed or a legitimate shortage of cash available to pay the agreed upon commission. If there's no apparent legitimate reason for not paying the commission, then it's probably motivated by greed on the part of the seller who may be trying to work a little bit better deal at the last minute. If there appears to be a legitimate reason for a cash shortfall (e.g., a previously unknown liability that must be paid or increased inventory level or missing/unacceptable assets that the buyer won't pay for), the broker may accept a deferred commission to ensure the Closing takes place. The broker should be given an appropriate short term Promissory Note for the difference from the seller. A business broker probably will not allow a Closing to fail because of an unwillingness to compromise in a legitimately unexpected situation.

Closing Checklist

The following is a sample checklist that may be helpful to you as you prepare for your business closing. It's representative of a broad range of situations but needs to be refined to fit your particular business transaction. It's a good idea to prepare your own customized closing checklist with a timeline to make sure all of the bases are covered for your unique closing and no unpleasant surprises are discovered at the last minute.

- ❏ Are all financing arrangements accomplished and the related documentation prepared and approved including mortgages and Promissory Notes?

- ❏ Have all of the necessary funds to be transferred at the closing been deposited with the escrow agent, including all monies due to the seller, the broker, the attorneys, and the payoff amounts for any liens and mortgages to be retired, and taxes to be paid?

❑ Have all leases, sub-leases, and other real property issues been resolved and the necessary documents prepared for assignment?

❑ Are all licenses, permits, approvals, and other official government requirements been taken care of?

❑ Has the necessary compliance with the state's Bulk Sales Law been accomplished?

❑ Have the attorneys involved prepared all of the necessary legal documentation to transfer the ownership of the business in accordance with the terms and conditions of the Purchase and Sale Agreement? For example; real estate deeds, employment contracts, covenants, contract of sale, equipment leases, assignments, security agreements, etc.

❑ Has the buyer prepared and submitted a business plan for the seller's review and approval (if the seller is financing the sale of the business)?

❑ Has a final inventory been taken and approved by the buyer and agreed to by the seller?

❑ Has a final inspection of the assets to be transferred as part of the business sale been accomplished by the buyer and agreed to by the seller?

❑ Have all of the business's outstanding liens and liabilities been addressed for extinguishment or assignment?

❑ Have the broker and seller resolved and agreed to the commission fee due to the broker as compensation for services rendered?

❑ If the business is a franchise, have all of the necessary Franchiser approvals and assignments been received?

❑ If the business is to be sold as a corporation, have all of the stockholder and director approvals and resolutions been enacted?

❑ Are all of the other related documents finalized such as the seller's post-sale employment agreement, the buyer's financial statements, equipment lists, inventory list, customer list, patent rights assignment, trade name and/or trademark assignments, and copyright assignments?

❑ Have all of the necessary keys, lock combinations, passwords, equipment warranties, etc. been inventoried and prepared for transfer to the buyer?

Post-Sale And Other Issues

- *Take Possession Of The Business*
- *Maintain The Status Quo*
- *Other Important Steps To Take*
- *Preparing A Business Plan*
- *Help After The Business Sale*
- *In Summary*

Take Possession Of The Business

It may seem obvious, but I'll state it anyway because there may be more to it than you think. The first thing the buyer does after the closing is to take possession of the business! This may include the following considerations:

- Change the locks on the business property.

- Formally notify employees (they may already know, but a clear starting point for the new owner is important).

- Notify the suppliers.

- Notify the customers (if appropriate to the type of business).

- File all new legal paperwork with the proper authorities (titles, licenses, liens, etc.).

- Etc., etc.

Maintain The Status Quo

Early in this chapter is an appropriate place for another important law of the jungle:

Strategic Jungle Law #13:

"After buying a business, don't change anything at first!"

Of course, this doesn't hold true if you're buying a turnaround situation; but in general, if the business you're buying is profitable, leave it alone while you learn how to manage it in accordance with the status quo.

One of the experiences I've had that best illustrates this point is as follows:

> One buyer of an operating fast food chicken business franchise soon after the closing changed chicken meat suppliers because he found that he could get the chicken at 10¢ a pound cheaper. What the new owner didn't realize was that these chicken pieces were 25% larger than those provided by the original supplier. The franchise doesn't sell chicken by the pound; it sells it by the piece. The new franchise owner completely wiped out his profit margin by paying a smaller price per pound but delivering to the customer 25% more chicken at the same retail price!

Other Important Steps To Take

The buyer should continue working with the seller, if at all possible, because it's very important in most businesses to have a consulting agreement worked out to retain the seller's services for a period of time after the sale. In fact, you can structure this agreement as part of the selling price of the business during negotiations. The buyer may need the seller's continuing advice after the sale to explain the million and one things that will come up later, but were never discussed prior to the sale.

The buyer should contact all of the business's customers if at all feasible to make an introduction and to assure them that things will remain running as well or better than before. The new owner certainly doesn't want any nervous customers jumping ship right after the business changes hands because they don't know what to expect.

The buyer should contact all current suppliers to the business to assure them that for the time being all arrangements will remain the same and to ensure that all accounts payable arrangements (if favorable) remain in place.

If the seller has taken back a mortgage in the business, close contact with the new business owner should be maintained to help smooth any rough spots to ensure the success of the new owner. Remember, an unsuccessful buyer will most likely just walk away from the business, and the seller may have no way of collecting the money owed and may be left with a ruined business which will have to be rebuilt or dissolved.

The buyer should immediately file information with the local municipality that the business has changed hands, and the new owner should file a new "d/b/a" (doing business as) to establish a continuing right to use the business name.

Preparing A Business Plan

Although a buyer should have already prepared a business plan long before the actual purchase of a business, most buyers don't do so unless they're forced to by a commercial lending institution as a prerequisite for financing. Sellers who are themselves financing the sale of their business should require that the buyer prepare a business plan for the seller's review and approval prior to the closing. This will help to ensure that the buyer will be taking a reasonable, well-planned approach to running the newly acquired business. After all, the seller doesn't want the buyer to default and return the ruined business.

Even though a carefully prepared business plan is clearly important to both the buyer and seller, it usually isn't done prior to the actual sale of the business. Therefore, I've chosen to include a discussion of this important point in this chapter. If you are about to, or have just purchased an operating business and you haven't yet written a business plan, do it now! Sellers may also find that if they have a well thought out and documented business plan to offer to a buyer during the negotiation process, it may help to build value in the buyer's mind.

Why Even Prepare a Plan?

The business plan is a written summary of what is hoped to be accomplished by the business and how it's intended to organize the resources to meet the goals. It's the road map for operating the business and most importantly should form the basis for measuring progress along the way. This brings up the next law of the jungle:

Strategic Jungle Law #14:

"You'll never get there if you don't know where you're going!"

- The business plan identifies the amount of financing or outside investment required and when it's needed.

- A well-organized plan is essential for a lender or investor to assess a financing proposal and to assess the quality of business management.

- By committing plans to paper, the overall ability to manage the business will improve. Business owners will be able to concentrate their efforts on the deviations from the plan before conditions become serious problems. They'll also have time to look ahead and avoid problems before they arise.

- It encourages realism in the projections for the business.

- It helps to identify the business's customers, the business market area, the pricing strategy, and the competitive conditions under which a business must operate to succeed. This process often leads to the discovery of a competitive advantage or new opportunity.

- A few hours spent each month updating the plan will save time and money in the long run and may even save the business. Firmly resolve now to make planning a part of your business management.

A business plan can be in any format that best suits the particular business's purposes, but as a minimum, the plan should include the following sections:

- Executive Summary
- Business Concept
- Description of the Business's Industry
- Description of the Business Venture
- Business Goals
- Marketing Plan
- Sales Forecast
- Production Plan
- Business Legal Structure
- Risk Assessment
- Action Plan and Milestone Chart
- Financial Plan, Statements, and Forecasts
- Financing and Capitalization Plan
- Operating Loans
- References

Executive Summary

The format should start with an executive summary describing the highlights of the business plan. Even though the entire business plan is well described later in the body of the plan, a crisp, one or two page introduction helps to capture the reader's immediate attention:

- Business name (include trade name, corporate name, and "doing business as" name, if appropriate, and address and phone number)

- Contact person (key person's name, title, and phone number)

- Short description of the business (nature of business and market area)

- Securities to be offered to investors (preferred shares, common shares, etc.)

- Business loans sought (bank loan, operating line of credit, seller financing, etc.)

- Highlights of the business plan (the objectives, the competitive advantage and "bottom line" in a short, concise form)

Business Concept

The business concept identifies the business's market potential within its industry and outlines the business's action plan for at least the coming year. Make sure the stated business goals are compatible with the owner's personal goals, the owner's management ability, and family considerations.

An important part of the business concept is the business monthly sales forecast for the coming year. It's the business's statement of confidence in a marketing strategy and forms the basis for the cash flow forecast and projected income statement.

The business concept contains an assessment of business risks and a contingency plan for dealing with those risks. Being honest about business risks and how to deal with them is important to the potential success of the business and is evidence of sound management.

Description of the Business's Industry

Provide a general overview of the pertinent industry in which the business operates. Include the following:

- Industry outlook and growth potential (include industry trends, new products and developments. It's best to include sources of information)

- Markets and customers (size of total market, new requirements and market trends)

- Competition (market share, strengths and weaknesses, estimated profitability)

- National and economic trends (population shifts, consumer trends, relevant economic indicators)

Description of the Business Venture

It's in this section where you describe what it is that the business sells and how the business obtains its products and services. This is a very important section, and is also very important to the business that it be carefully considered. There's an old maxim that I'll use here as the 15th and last law of the jungle:

Strategic Jungle Law #15:

"You can't sell from an empty wagon!"

This means that you must have products or valuable services to sell or you won't have a business. The key items within this section of the business plan are:

- Product(s) or service to be provided

- Product protection/exclusive rights (patents, copyrights, trademarks, trade names, franchise rights)

- Target market (typical customers identified by groups, buying patterns and average purchase in dollars, wants and needs)

- Competitive advantage of the business concept (the market niche, uniqueness, estimated market share)

- Business location, size, and other physical characteristics

- Staff and equipment needed (overall requirement, capacity)

Business Goals

You should give careful consideration to the business goals and how they may change as the business comes under new ownership. You should include:

- One year (specific goals, such as gross sales, profit margins, share of market, opening new store, plant or office, introducing new product, etc.)

- Over the longer term (return on investment, business net worth, sale of business, etc.)

Marketing Plan

- Sales strategy (include commissioned sales staff, agents, sales objectives, target customers, sales tools, sales support)

- Distribution of product or service (direct to public, wholesale, retail, multiple outlets)

- Pricing (costing, mark-ups, margins, break-even points)

- Promotion (media advertising, publicity, etc.)

- Guarantees (product guarantees, service warranties)

- Tracking methods (method for confirming who the business's customers are and how they heard about the business)

Sales Forecast

- Assumptions (all the assumptions made in developing the forecast)

- Monthly forecast for coming year (sales volume in units and dollars)

- Annual forecast for following two to four years (sales volume in dollars)

Production Plan (Manufacturing)

- Brief description of production process

- Physical plant requirements (building layout and characteristics, utility requirements, expansion capability, etc.)

- Machinery and equipment (new or used, lease or purchase, capacity)

- Raw materials (availability, quality, sources)

- Inventory requirements (seasonal levels, turnover rates, method of control)

- Suppliers (volume discounts, multiple sources)

- Personnel required (full-time, part-time, skill level, availability, training required)

- Cost of facilities, equipment, and materials (estimates and quotes)

- Capital estimates (one time start-up or expansion capital required)

Production Plan (Retail or Service)

- Purchasing plans (volume discounts, multiple sources, quality, price)

- Inventory system (seasonal variation, turnover rates, methods of control)

- Space requirements (retail floor and office space, improvement required, expansion capability)

- Staff and equipment required (personnel by skill level, fixtures, office equipment)

Business Legal Structure

- Legal form (proprietorship, partnership, corporation, other)

- Share distribution (list of principal shareholders, if incorporated)

- List of contracts and agreements in force (management contract, shareholder or partnership agreement, franchise agreement, service contract)

- Directors and officers (names and addresses and role in the business)

- Background of key management personnel and other principals involved (brief resumes of active owners and key employees)

- Contract professionals/consultants (possible outside assistance in specialized or deficient areas)

- Organization chart (identify reporting relationships)

- Duties and responsibilities of key personnel (brief job descriptions – who is responsible for what?)

Risk Assessment

- Competitors' expected reaction to new business ownership

- Analysis of critical external factors (identify effects of possible strikes, recession, new technology, weather, new competition, supplier problems, shifts in consumer demand, etc.)

- Analysis of critical internal factors (sales decline, sales increase, loss of key manager, workers unionize)

- Dealing with risks (contingency plan to handle the most significant risks)

Action Plan and Milestone Chart

- Steps to accomplish this year's goals (flow chart by month or by quarter of specific action to be taken and by whom)

- Checkpoints for measuring results (identify significant dates, sales levels, production levels as decision points)

Financial Plan

The financial plan is usually a concise outline of the level of present financial operations. It also contains pro-forma financial forecasts. In carrying out the business's action plan for the coming year, these operating forecasts are a guide to business survival and profitability. You should refer to them often during the operation of the business and, if circumstances dictate, re-work them as necessary.

Financial Statements

- Previous year's balance sheets and income and expense statements (include past two to three years if applicable from business being purchased)

Financial Forecasts

- Opening balance sheet (for the start of the new business ownership)

- Projected income statements (detailed operating forecast for the next year of operation and less detailed forecast for the following two years)

- Cash flow forecast (budget of cash inflow and outflow on a monthly basis for next year of operation)

Financing and Capitalization Plan

- Loans applied for including Promissory Notes to be given to the business seller (amount, term, payment schedule)

- Purpose of loan (attach a detailed description of assets to be financed with cost quotations)

- Owner's equity (your level of financial commitment to the business)

- Summary of loan requirements (for a particular asset or for the business as a whole)

Operating Loan

- Line of credit applied for and security offered

- Maximum operating cash requirement

References

- Name of present lending institution (branch, type of accounts)

- Attorney's name (include address and phone number)

- Accountant's name (include address and phone number)

Appendices

The following documents are important to be provided as appendices to the business plan:

- Personal net worth statement of the principals (including personal property values, investments, cash, bank loans, charge accounts, mortgages, other liabilities).

- Letters of business intent (potential orders, customer commitments, letters of support)

- List of inventory (type, age, value)

- List of leasehold improvements (description, when accomplished)

- List of fixed assets (description, age)

- Price lists (to support cost estimates)

- Description of insurance coverage (insurance policies, amount of coverage)

- Accounts receivable summary (if being purchased as part of the business)

- Accounts payable summary (if being purchased as part of the business)

- Copies of legal agreements (contracts, lease, franchise agreement, mortgage)

- Appraisals (real estate, furniture, fixtures, and equipment)

Help After The Business Sale

For free help in preparing a business and/or a marketing plan, the local office of the Small Business Administration's Small Business Development Center (SBDC) is a great resource as is the Service Corps of Retired Executives (SCORE). Look in your telephone book for the office nearest you or if you're Internet savvy you can go on-line at **http://www.sba.gov** to get SBDC office locations as well as other information and help.

There are many other sources of help and assistance that new business owners can look to as they begin their new undertaking. I'll provide a few of them here for your consideration:

- Many local colleges and universities have continuing education programs targeted specifically towards small business.

- You may want to join local merchant and/or trade groups. They frequently help each other in many ways through sharing information, jointly buying supplies and advertising, and participating in group insurance programs.

- Don't overlook your suppliers as sources of help and advice. They have a vested interest in seeing you succeed and continuing as a customer/client.

- There are usually many very informative one-day seminars put on in the larger cities by several different national training companies. They address everything from understanding and using computers to the full gamut of small business operations.

- Plan to attend as many industry conferences and trade shows as you can. These events will keep you aware of what's going on within your industry and will give you additional opportunities to establish business relationships with other similar business owners and suppliers.

- The local Chamber of Commerce is also usually a good source of information about help with getting a business started. They'll be able to refer you to a local professional who may be willing to help you "pro bono" in hope of attracting you as a future customer.

The following are some good sources of information for new business owners or those wanting to get into business for the first time:

National SCORE Office
409 3rd Street SW, Suite 5900
Washington, DC 20024
800-634-0245
http://www.score.org

Small Business Develop. Centers
8990 Burke Lake Road
Burke, VA 22015
703-764-9850
http://www.asbdc-us.org

U.S. Small Business Admin.
Small Business Directory
PO Box 1000
Fort Worth, TX 76119
800-827-5722
http://www.sba.gov

U. S. Small Business Admin.
SBA Publications
PO Box 30
Denver, CO 80201
http://www.sba.gov

U.S. Patent & Trademark Office
Crystal Plaza 3, Room 2C02
Washington, DC 20231
800-786-9199
http://www.uspto.gov

U.S. Chamber of Commerce
1615 H St. NW
Washington, DC 20062
202-659-6000
http://www.uschamber.org

National Minority Business Council
25 W 45th St.
New York, NY 10017
212-997-4753
http://www.nmbc.org

National Assoc. for the Self-Employed
2121 Precinct Line Rd.
Hurst, TX 76054
800-232-6273
http://www.nase.org

National Fed. of Independent Business
1201 F St. NW Suite 200
Washington, DC 20004
202-554-9000
http://www.nfib.com

Nat'l Assoc. Women Business Owners
1595 Spring Hill Road Suite 330
Vienna, VA 22182
703-506-3268
http://www.nawbo.org

In Summary

This chapter concludes this book that has provided you with a complete overview of the complicated process of buying and selling a business. By now, you should know about dealing with brokers, finding business buyers and sellers, valuing an operating profitable business, conducting negotiations, and closing the deal. It's my sincere hope that this book has been of value to you in helping to de-mystify the business buying and selling process. Of course, no one book can be all things to all people. I recommend that you seek additional information in any area you feel a need for more extensive treatment of the subject matter. As a matter of information, The Business Book Press at www.BusinessBookPress.com provides additional resources which will provide more in-depth and detailed discussion of the business buying, selling and valuation process as well as detailed strategies for a seller to prepare their business for sale for the most money.

I welcome any comments and/or suggestions about this book that you may have. I'll even be happy to personally try to answer any questions for you about buying or selling a business that I haven't addressed or which are unique to your particular circumstance. Just write or e-mail me in care of the publisher at rds@businessbookpress.com.

Good luck to all of you buyers and sellers, and remember, it's the fair deal rather than the best deal that will most likely make all of you successful!

Russell L. Brown
Author

Strategic Laws Of The Business Buying And Selling Jungle

"Example Only"

Hold Harmless Agreement

The Seller of the business known as _____

(hereinafter referred to as "the Business") located at _____

_____

hereby agrees to indemnify the Buyer of the Business against and in respect of any and all liabilities or obligations of or claims against the Business of any nature, whether accrued, absolute, contingent, or otherwise, existing or asserted to exist as of the closing date to the extent the liability, obligation, or claim is not disclosed on the Schedule attached hereto as of the date of this Agreement; and any and all losses, damages, costs, and expenses incurred by the Buyer in defending against any of those matters or by reason of any breach of any of the representations and warranties of the Seller made in the Business Purchase and Sale Agreement or in any certificate, document, or other instrument delivered pursuant to the purchase of the Business.

IN WITNESS WHEREOF, the parties have executed this Agreement at

_____ on _____ .

Date

_____ **BUYER** _____
Witness   Signature

_____   _____
Witness   Printed or typed Name

_____ **SELLER** _____
Witness   Signature

_____   _____
Witness   Printed or typed name

"Example Only"
Earnest Money Agreement/Letter of Intent

Received from _____, Buyer, the sum of

_____ in the form of

( ) cash, ( ) check payable to _____ which sum

represents earnest money in part payment for the purchase of the business known as: _____

_____

and located at: _____

1. The business to be purchased is more fully described as follows: (see Attachment)

2. The purchase price is _____ subject to the approval of Seller and
   is payable as follows:

       Earnest money, receipt of which is hereby acknowledged: $_____

       Upon execution of the Purchase and Sale Agreement: $_____

       At the time of closing in cash or certified funds: $_____

       At the time of closing by promissory note: $_____

3. Rights to be assigned such as; patents, copyrights, trade names, etc. (see Attachment)

4. Special terms between Seller and Buyer: (see Attachment)

5. Other Terms:

     (a) A Purchase and Sale Agreement will be entered into on or before _____, 20_____

     (b) The closing shall take place on or before _____, 20_____,
   at the offices of Seller's attorney.

This document when signed by Seller, shall bind the parties until superseded by a written Purchase and Sale Agreement incorporating the terms hereof.

IN WITNESS WHEREOF, the parties hereto hereby agree that they have read, approve, and accept the above terms and conditions and have hereunto set their hands this _____ day of _____, 20_____.

Sign here if Buyer
is an individual
or partnership: _____
                Buyer

Sign here if Seller
is an individual
or partnership: _____
                Seller

Sign here if Buyer
is a Corporation: _____
                Buyer

Sign here if Seller
is a Corporation: _____
                Seller

"Example Only"

Confidentiality Agreement

This will acknowledge that on the date as set forth below I have received from

_____certain pertinent, confidential,

and proprietary information relating to the sale of the following business:

        BUSINESS NAME: _____

             ADDRESS: _____

                                  _____

Specifically, I have received the following informational documentation:

_____

_____

_____

I understand that this information has been disclosed solely for my own consideration in negotiations concerning the possible purchase of the above named business. Further, I agree that said information will be held in strict confidence by myself and not divulged to others with the exception of my duly authorized attorney and accountant. In the event that I do not purchase the business, I will agree not to disclose any of the information provided to me or that I learn during negotiations, directly or indirectly, including the fact that the business is for sale, for a period of at least three (3) years from the date hereof.

IN WITNESS WHEREOF, the parties have executed this Agreement at _____

on _____.

Buyer's
Name:_____ Sign_____ Date _____
                    print or type

Witness
Name:_____ Sign_____ Date _____
                    print or type

Witness
Name:_____ Sign_____ Date _____
                    print or type

"Example Only"

Buyer's Financial Qualification Statement

Name: _____

Address: _____

Telephone: _____ Own Home? _____

Years at this address: _____ Years at previous address _____

Location and description of real estate owned (other than residence):

_____

_____

Cash available for business purchase: $ _____

Sources of cash and financing for the business purchase:

_____

_____

_____

Credit references (include banks, charge card accounts, etc.):

_____

_____

_____

Names and locations of previously owned business(es):

_____

_____

_____

Append any personal financial information statements

Buyer's Financial Qualification Statement
(continued)

Have you ever declared bankruptcy?   YES _____   NO _____

If yes, complete: Date declared _____

State in which declared _____

Date bankruptcy resolved _____

I, _____ (Business Seller) of _____

_____ (address) on this date _____

agree to use the financial information contained in this Statement solely for the purposes of establishing the financial viability of the above named person in the potential sale of

_____

I, _____ (Business Buyer) on this date _____
certify that to my best belief and knowledge, all of the information provided on and appended to this form is true, and I authorize the above named Business Seller to use this information solely for the purpose of considering my financial capability of potentially purchasing the Business known as

_____

IN WITNESS WHEREOF, the parties have executed this Statement at _____

on _____ .

_____   **BUYER** _____
          Witness   Signature

_____   _____
          Witness   Printed or typed Name

_____   **SELLER** _____
          Witness   Signature

_____   _____
          Witness   Printed or typed name

"Example Only"

Covenant Not To Compete Agreement

In consideration of the payments provided for the business known as _____

_____ (hereinafter referred to as "the Business") located at _____

_____, the Seller covenants that for a period of

_____ from the date of this Covenant, the Seller shall not, directly or

indirectly, within a radius of _____ miles of _____ (Seller's place of business),

individually or in association with or as agent or employee of or as an investor in any part-

nership or corporation, engage in the business of selling _____

_____ or other products and/or services of substantially the same kind or

character and to the same class of trade as sold by Seller at any time during the _____

(month/year) period preceding this date. In particular, but by way of limiting and defining

the foregoing, the Seller shall not solicit any of the Seller's customers for the purchase of

such products and/or services within this area during that period.

IN WITNESS WHEREOF, the parties have executed this Agreement at

_____ on _____
                                              Date

_____ **BUYER** _____
             Witness   Signature

_____   _____
             Witness   Printed or typed Name

                                           SELLER _____
_____   Signature
             Witness

_____   _____
             Witness   Printed or typed name

"Example Only"

Business Purchase and Sale Agreement

AGREEMENT made on _____ 20_____ by _____

having a principal place of business at _____

(hereinafter referred to as the Business Seller) d/b/a _____

(hereinafter referred to as the Business) and _____ of

_____(hereinafter referred to as the Business Buyer).

RECITALS

WHEREAS, the Business Seller presently owns and desires to sell the business known as

_____ and is situated at

_____; and

WHEREAS, the Business Buyer desires to purchase the Business;

NOW THEREFORE, in consideration of the mutual covenants and obligations set out herein, the parties agree as follows:

ARTICLE ONE — SALE OF BUSINESS

Business Seller shall sell, assign, and deliver to Business Buyer, and Business Buyer shall purchase and accept, on the closing date, all assets and goodwill of the Business, excluding _____, owned by the Business Seller or in which the Business Seller has any right, title, or interest, all as more specifically described as follows:

(a) The trademarked name: _____

(b) All properly functioning computer software, programs, disks and any other material specifically tailored to produce: _____

(c) All rights to unconditionally continue to operate the Business indefinitely in _____ _____ and any other business conducted by the Business at any time in the past or any other business approach the Business Buyer may wish to pursue in the future.

(d) A full and complete listing of all names, addresses, and telephone numbers for all current and past customers for the past two (2) years.

(e) All remaining inventory consisting of: _____ and any other items pertinent to the operation of the Business.

(f) All furniture, fixtures, and equipment more fully described in Attachment _____

(g) All patents, trade names, copyrights, and proprietary information more fully described in Attachment _____

ARTICLE TWO — CONSIDERATION; ASSUMPTION OF LIABILITIES

In consideration of the sale of the assets under this Agreement and of all other things done and agreed to be done by Business Seller hereunder, with the exclusion of Article Thirteen - Post Closing Service Agreement, Business Buyer shall pay to Business Seller on the closing date of the sum of $_____ and shall assume no liabilities of the Business Seller.

ARTICLE THREE — INSTRUMENTS OF TRANSFER

The transfers to be made to Business Buyer pursuant to this Agreement shall be effected by a Bill of Sale. The Business Seller shall prepare a Bill of Sale that recites and adequately identifies the assets and personal property transferred and conveyed to the Business Buyer in accordance with this Agreement.

ARTICLE FOUR — ASSIGNMENT OF CONTRACT RIGHTS

If any contract, license, commitment, subscription, or sales or purchase order assignable to Business Buyer hereunder may not be assigned without the consent of the other party thereto, Business Seller shall use its best efforts to obtain the consent of the other party to such assignment.

ARTICLE FIVE — ACCOUNTS RECEIVABLE

After the closing date, Business Buyer shall have the authority to collect all receivables transferred to the Business Buyer hereunder and to endorse without recourse and without warranties of any kind the name of Business Seller on any checks or evidence of indebtedness received by Business Buyer on account of any such receivables. Business Seller shall transfer and deliver to Business Buyer any cash or other property that Business Seller may receive in respect to any such receivables after the closing date.

ARTICLE SIX — CLOSING

The closing shall take place on _____ 19_____ at _____(time) at the offices of

_____or at such other time and

place as the parties agree upon in writing.

ARTICLE SEVEN — REPRESENTATIONS AND WARRANTIES OF BUSINESS SELLER

Business Seller represents, warrants, and agrees:

(a) That the Business is a wholly owned asset of _____ duly organized, existing, and in good standing under the laws of the State of _____, and is authorized and entitled to carry on its business in _____ [state]. The execution and delivery of this Agreement by the Business Seller further warrants that the Business is wholly and singly owned and no encumbrances of any kind to the sale of the Business do now or will exist at the time of closing. The execution and delivery of this Agreement by the Business Seller has been duly authorized by its Board of Directors and by its Shareholders in accordance with the By-Laws of the corporation.

(b) At least ten (10) days before the closing date, the Business Seller shall furnish to the Business Buyer an accurate and complete list of all tangible assets relating to the Business, all of which are free and clear of all mortgages, liens, and encumbrances.

(c) The Business Seller is not a party to any Business related employment agreement, agreement for the future purchase of materials, supplies, or equipment, or sales agreement, or subscription agreement, that relates to any period beyond the closing date, whether written or oral, except as otherwise listed below:

_____

_____

_____

_____

(d) Business Seller is not in default under any contract, agreement, lease or other document to which it is a party and has complied with all laws, regulations, and ordinances applicable to its business to the date of this Agreement.

(e) The Business Seller's obligations to its paid customers as of the date of this Agreement are as follows:

_____

_____

_____

_____

(f) The Business Buyer assumes no liabilities of Business Seller other than those specifically recited herein and Business Seller indemnifies and holds Business Buyer harmless from any and all such unassumed liabilities.

(g) There are no judgments, liens, actions, or proceedings pending relating to this sale against the Business Seller or this Business in any court.

ARTICLE EIGHT — CONDITIONS PRECEDENT TO BUYER'S OBLIGATIONS

The obligations of Business Buyer under this Agreement are conditioned on the following all having occurred on or before the closing date:

(a) All actions, proceedings, instruments, and documents required of Business Seller under this agreement shall be in a form approved by counsel for Business Buyer, provided that such approval shall not be unreasonably withheld.

(b) The representations and warranties made by Business Seller herein shall be substantially correct on the closing date, except as affected by transactions contemplated herein and changes occurring in the ordinary course of business, with the same force and effect as though such representations and warranties had been made on the closing date.

(c) The instruments executed and delivered to Business Buyer by Business Seller pursuant to this Agreement are valid in accordance with their terms, and effectively vest in Business Buyer good and marketable title to the assets and Business as contemplated by this agreement, free and clear of any liabilities, obligations, and encumbrances, except those liabilities and obligations expressly assumed by Business Buyer as provided herein:

ARTICLE NINE — COVENANT NOT TO COMPETE

Except in the event of a default on the part of the Business Buyer of any of the provisions of this Agreement, for a period continuing for two (2) years after the closing date, Business Seller shall not, directly or indirectly, engage in any business involving the ownership, management, or operation of _____

_____

in the State(s)of _____

ARTICLE TEN — EXPENSES OF NEGOTIATION AND TRANSFER

Each party shall pay its own expenses, taxes, and other costs incident to or resulting from this Agreement, whether or not the transactions contemplated herein are consummated.

ARTICLE ELEVEN — CONDUCT OF BUSINESS

Prior to closing, Business Seller shall carry on business in the usual and ordinary manner to and including the closing date of the sale, if any, or any extension of such date, but shall not enter into any unusual contracts or make any unusual commitments affecting the operation of the business beyond such closing date without the consent of Business Buyer. During the term of this Agreement, Business Buyer, through Business Buyer's agents and representatives, shall have full and complete access, at all reasonable times with prior notice, to the premises and to all the books and records of the Business Seller.

ARTICLE TWELVE — LICENSE OF TRADE NAMES

The Business Seller hereby transfers to the Business Buyer its entire right, title, interest in and use of the trade name "_____" and any corresponding trademarks, logos, or copyrights. Additionally, the Business Buyer is authorized to refer to the Business as "_____". Further, the Business Buyer is authorized to refer to the founder/previous owner _____, in various ways in sales and promotion literature and to reprint and use any and all previously used promotional material that has been used in the past by the Business and/or the Business Seller.

ARTICLE THIRTEEN — POST CLOSING
SERVICE AGREEMENT

The Business Seller agrees to provide to the Business Buyer, within 30 days after the closing date, at a time established by the Business Buyer, full training, guidance, direction, and counseling sufficient for the business operation using all tools, techniques, information sources, mailing lists, ordering fulfillment services, and any other necessary functions. All costs and resultant revenues associated with this usage will be borne and realized by the Business Buyer. Fulfillment of this condition will be in accordance with the current and normal methods and locations of the business. The Business Seller will be paid the total sum of $_____ for services rendered upon completion of this service agreement.

ARTICLE FOURTEEN — NOTICES

Notices to be given or served hereunder shall be in writing and shall be deemed duly served if delivered personally or mailed by certified mail to the following addresses:

(a) Notices to Business Seller:

_____

_____

_____

_____

(b) Notices to Business Buyer:

_____

_____

_____

_____

ARTICLE FIFTEEN – COOPERATION OF THE PARTIES

All of the parties shall, at any time and from time to time, sign and deliver any documents that may be necessary or desirable to effectuate or implement any of the provisions of this Agreement on request of the other party.

ARTICLE SIXTEEN – MODIFICATION

No modification or amendment of this Agreement shall be effective unless such modification or amendment is in writing and signed by all of the parties hereto.

ARTICLE SEVENTEEN – SUCCESSION AND SURVIVAL OF RIGHTS

This Agreement shall be binding upon and inure to the benefit of the parties hereto and their respective heirs, representatives, executors, administrators, successors and assigns. All terms, covenants, conditions and agreements contained herein shall survive the delivery and acceptance of the assets and property transferred pursuant to this Agreement.

ARTICLE EIGHTEEN — APPLICABLE LAW

This Agreement has been made and entered into in the State of _____ and the laws of _____ shall govern the validity and interpretation of this Agreement and the performance due hereunder.

ARTICLE NINETEEN — ENTIRE AGREEMENT

This instrument contains the entire agreement between the parties with respect to the transaction contemplated herein. It may be executed in one or more counterparts, each of which shall be deemed an original, but all of which together shall constitute one and the same instrument.

ARTICLE TWENTY — MISCELLANEOUS PROVISIONS

The underlined captions set forth in this Agreement at the beginning of all articles are for convenience of reference only and shall not be deemed to define or limit the provisions hereof or to affect in any way their construction and application. When the context so requires, the masculine gender shall include the feminine, and the singular shall include the plural, and the plural, the singular.

IN WITNESS WHEREOF, the parties have executed this Agreement at

_____, the day and year first above written.

_____
Witness

BUYER _____
Signature

_____
Witness

_____
Printed or typed Name

_____
Witness

SELLER _____
Signature

_____
Witness

_____
Printed or typed name

Glossary of General Terms
Common to the Purchase and Sale
of an Operating Business

The following is a glossary of common terms that you'll probably run across in buying or selling a business. I've selected the terms described in this glossary to those primarily associated with the purchase and sale of business assets, although many of the terms associated with the purchase and sale of a corporation are also included.

Accounting: The process of recording financial activities of a business, summarizing these activities, and analyzing the results.

Accounts payable: An obligation by a business to pay an amount to a vendor or other creditor for goods and services purchased on credit.

Accounts receivable: A financial claim by a business against a customer arising from a sale of goods or services on credit. One measure of the health of a business is how fast customers pay off their accounts. Less than 30 days is good, 30 to 60 days may be okay, and over 60 days could be a problem.

Accounting cost: The process of collecting material, labor, and overhead costs and allocating them to products.

Accounting period: The period of time over which a business's income and expense statement summarizes changes (usually based on a fiscal year).

Accrued interest: Unpaid interest to date on a note or mortgage.

Accrued liabilities and expenses: Accumulated charges, such as interest or taxes, owed but not yet billed to the business, and therefore, not yet paid.

Accumulated depreciation: The total depreciation of an asset that has been charged as an expense to date.

Acid-test ratio: Also known as the "quick" ratio, it's the amount of current assets less the inventory, and divided by current liabilities; the standard is 1:1 and is a good snapshot indication of the health of the business. A business certainly needs enough current income to at least balance current expenses or it will be quickly in trouble.

Amortization:	A spreading out of costs over a period of time similar to depreciation. For example, it can be a reduction in a debt or fund by periodic payments covering interest and part of the principal over a period of time. It's different from depreciation in that depreciation usually refers to physical things where amortization applies to things that expire (mortgages, patents, etc.).
Amortization schedule:	A tabular presentation of the reduction in value of something being amortized.
Assessed valuation:	The taxable value of an asset as determined by a governmental source.
Assets:	Everything a company owns or is due to it: current assets, such as cash, investments, money due, materials, and inventories; fixed assets, such as land, buildings (real estate), and machinery; and intangible assets, such as patents, and other goodwill.
Asset, current:	An asset which is either currently in the form of cash or is expected to be converted into cash within a short period, usually less than one year.
Asset, fixed:	Tangible physical property of relatively long life that generally is used in the production of goods and services.
Asset, intangible:	Assets which normally have no physical form such as: skilled employees, patents, trade names, good standing in the community, etc.
Asset, net book value of:	Original cost of the asset less the accumulated depreciation.
Asset purchase:	The process of buying a business's specified assets rather than purchasing its common stock.
Audited Financial Statements:	A business's financial statements that have been prepared by a certified public accountant (CPA) independent of the business owner in accordance with generally accepted accounting principles. These statements show the business's financial position and its results of operations.
Available Cash Flow:	The estimated actual cash available to a business owner after elimination of non-cash expenses (e.g. depreciation) and discretionary expenses (e.g. excess wages, donations, interest, etc.).

Balance Sheet:	A statement showing the nature and amount of a business's assets, liabilities, and equity on a given date. In dollar amounts, the balance sheet shows what the business owned, what it owed, and the ownership interest in the company of its owners.
Base year:	A year chosen for comparison of numbers as the 100%, or "normal", year from which index numbers are computed.
Book Value (of an asset):	The accounting value of an asset shown on the Balance Sheet that's the original cost of the asset less its accumulated depreciation. Keep in mind that this value may have little or no relationship to the real market value of the asset. Frequently, depreciation expenses are charged much faster than the actual decline in the asset's market value.
Book Value (of a business):	The book value of a business is determined from the financial records, by adding the current value of all assets (generally excluding such intangibles as goodwill), then deducting all debts and other liabilities. Book value of the business may have little or no significant relationship to actual market value due to depreciation and a lack of consideration for goodwill (intangible assets).
Break-even point:	This is the point at which a business's net sales revenue equals its total costs. A quick look calculation for the business's break-even point is: Sales revenue = total fixed costs ÷ gross margin of profit.
Bridge loan:	Usually a very short term loan of funds to cover an unusual expense or fall-off in revenues. Sometimes bridge loans are used by buyers of businesses to get them over the initial 30 to 90 day transition period of the changeover in ownership of a business.
Business Plan:	A written plan detailing a business's sales projections, expenses, marketing strategy, and objectives. A business plan is of great importance to anyone in business, but of paramount importance to anyone buying or starting a business. You'll never get there if you don't know where you're going!

Bulk Transfer:	Article 6 of the Uniform Commercial Code regulates the bulk transfer through the sale or ownership change of a large portion (usually greater than 50%) of a business's inventory, material, supplies, merchandise, and equipment. Requirements include the advance notification of creditors of the impending sale of a business and its assets listed above to prevent fraud. Provisions in each state are somewhat different so check your local statutes.
Capital:	The amount that an individual, partner, or stockholder has invested in a business; net worth of a business.
Capitalization:	The conversion of future income into a present value by use of a capitalization factor usually expressed as a percentage such as return on investment (ROI).
Capitalization (of an asset):	The accounting listing of an expenditure as a balance sheet asset rather than as an expense.
Capitalization (of a business):	The capital structure of a business consisting of the sum of the long term debt and the owner's equity.
Capitalization of Net Profit:	A process to determine the present value of a business by applying a capitalization rate (ROI) to the projected net profit of a business.
Capitalization Rate:	A percentage number used to determine the present value (today) of a stream of future earnings.
Cash Flow:	The difference between a business's cash receipts and its cash payments over a specific period of time.
Chattel Mortgage:	A financial claim on specifically identified personal property (non-real estate) to secure money owed on the property.
Closely Held Corporation:	An incorporated business whose corporate shares are held primarily by the principals in the business and are not publicly traded.
Closing:	The process of legally completing the purchase and sale of a business.
Collateral:	Assets pledged by a borrower to secure a loan repayment.

Commission:	The negotiated fee, usually a percentage of the purchase and sale price of the total business asset value, earned by a business broker for facilitating the sale of a business. Sometimes the value of the inventory and other non-capitalized assets are excluded from the calculation of the commission.
Common Stock:	Shares of ownership in a corporation.
Copyright:	A legal form of protection granted to authors of original works both through common law and through registration with the U.S. Copyright Office.
Corporation:	Entity or organization created by operation of law with rights of doing business essentially the same as those of an individual. The entity has continuous existence regardless of that of its owners and generally limits liability of owners to the amount invested in the organization. The entity ceases to exist only if dissolved according to proper legal process. It's easily transferred and has an unlimited life.
Cost of goods sold:	The price paid for the merchandise which has been sold by a business; beginning inventory plus net purchases minus ending inventory equals cost of goods sold.
Covenant Not To Compete:	An agreement given by the seller of a business to the business buyer to not compete in that or a similar business for a specified period of time, and within a specified geographic area.
Current assets:	Those assets of a business that are reasonably expected to be realized in cash, sold, or consumed during the normal operating cycle of the business. These include cash, U.S. Government bonds, accounts receivable, inventories, and short-term money due (usually within one year).
Current liabilities:	Money owed and payable by a business, usually within one year.
Current ratio:	The comparison of current assets to current liabilities which is the total current assets divided by total current liabilities. This ratio indicates a business's ability to pay its current debts with its current assets. A good ratio is 2:1.

Debt service:	This is the payment of principal and interest required on a debt (usually a loan or mortgage) over a specified period of time and interest rate.
Depreciation:	Charges against earnings to write off the cost, less salvage value, of an asset over its estimated useful life. It's a book-keeping entry for accounting and tax purposes and doesn't represent cash outlay.
Draw; owners:	Sometimes the owner of a small business (sole proprietor-ship or closely held corporation) will take income as a draw as opposed to a salary. The terms are essentially the same except that generally a salary means that all with-holding taxes, FICA, etc., are accounted for on the books of the business, whereas draw is straight cash to the owner who pays all tax obligations separately on a personal income tax return.
Due diligence:	The process of investigation by a potential buyer into the business's claimed financial and operational performance. This means reviewing actual IRS returns and/or audited financial statements, verifying inventory, verifying cus-tomers and sales, etc., in general, as a verification of any and all claims made by the business owner concerning the operation of the business to satisfy the buyer that all rep-resentations made are accurate.
Earnest money:	The deposit provided by a buyer to a seller as part of an offer to purchase a business under certain conditions. The money represents a serious intention to negotiate on the part of the potential buyer.
Earnings:	This is the same as income and profit.
Earnings Before Interest, Depreciation, Amortization (EBITDA):	The earnings of a business after eliminating non-cash expenses for depreciation and amortization, and after eliminating the discretionary expense of interest on debt.
Employment Agreement:	This is an agreement whereby key employees agree to remain with the business for a specified period of time under certain conditions.
Equity:	This is the net value of a business after all of the debts, claims, and assets are fully liquidated.

Expense allocation: The process of distributing an expense to a number of items or areas.

Factoring: A process used by some businesses to improve their cash flow. A factoring company (usually a finance company or a bank) pays to a business a certain portion of the business's trade debt and then is repaid as the trade debtors pay their account. This may be one more reason not to buy the accounts receivable; you don't have to find and clear any factoring liens.

Fictitious Name: A name frequently used by sole proprietors or partnerships to provide a business name, other than those of the owners or partners, under which the business will operate. Also known as the trade name and the "doing business as" (d/b/a) name.

Fiduciary: A position, or person in a position of trust upon which certain reliance of facts may be placed.

FIFO: The first in-first out method of inventory accounting that assumes that goods that enter the inventory first are the first to be sold.

Fiscal year: The annual accounting period selected by a business to best correspond to its operations. A fiscal year can correspond to a normal calendar year or begin/end anywhere in-between, e.g.; the Federal government's fiscal year begins 1 October and ends 30 September.

Franchise: A form of business organization in which the franchiser (the primary company) provides to a franchisee (the local business) a market tested business package involving a product or service. The franchisee operates under the franchiser's trade name and markets goods and/or services in accordance with a contractual agreement.

Goodwill: The collection of intangible assets represented in dollars by the difference between the total purchase price for the business and the net value of the tangible assets being purchased.

Gross margin: The gross profit of the business stated as a percentage of net sales revenue.

Gross profit (also gross income): The net sales revenue of the business minus the direct cost of the products sold or services provided.

Income, before taxes: Net sales minus cost of goods sold minus all expenses.

Income, net: Excess of total revenues over total expenses in a given period.

Income and Expense Statement: A summary of a business's revenues, expenses, and profits for a specific period of time, usually for a full fiscal year.

Installment sale The process of selling a business with the payments made over a period of time usually accompanied by a Promissory Note.

Intangible asset: A long-lived, non-physical asset, such as a patent, a copyright, or a trademark.

Inventory: Finished goods being held for sale, and raw material and partly finished products that upon completion will be sold by the business.

Inventory turnover: Total cost of goods sold divided by the average value of inventory. Some businesses have very high inventory turnover and generally work on very small product markups. Other businesses have low turnover (such as furniture stores, jewelry stores, major equipment manufacturers, etc.) and consequently, usually have significantly higher markups.

Key person insurance: This has forever been called "key man" insurance, but to be politically correct, I'll call it "key person." All this means is that the business is paying for the life insurance for key persons (usually the owner) with the business backers (partners, spouse, investors, etc.) as the beneficiaries. This protects the investors from a catastrophic loss. This is fully deductible and is sometimes used by small business owners as a way to get Uncle Sam to underwrite part of their personal life insurance premiums. It's frequently an add-back in a reconstruction of business expenses.

Lease: The agreement between parties for the rent of a particular asset (real estate, automobile, equipment, etc.).

Leasehold improvements: Usually refers to the improvements made by a lessee to a lessor's property. Generally, leasehold improvements may be capitalized by a business and depreciated against income, but ownership reverts to the lessor upon completion of the lease.

Lessee: The person or entity to which a lease of real or personal property is given.

Lessor: The person or entity giving a lease for real or personal property.

Liabilities: All the claims against a business. Liabilities can include accounts and wages and salaries payable, accrued taxes payable, and fixed or long-term liabilities, such as mortgage bonds, debentures, and bank loans.

Liability, current: Obligations against a business that become due within a short time, usually one year.

Lien: A legal claim on certain assets that are used to secure a loan.

Liquid assets: Those assets easily convertible into cash; marketable securities, receivables, checking and savings accounts, and cash itself.

Liquidation value: The market value of a business's tangible assets minus its liabilities under a forced sale.

Liquidity: A measure of the quality and adequacy of current assets to meet current obligations as they come due.

Long-term liability: A liability due at a time after the next business year.

Loss, net: Excess of total expenses over total revenues in a given period.

LIFO: The last-in-first-out method of inventory accounting that assumes goods that enter inventory last are the first to be sold.

Markup: The amount added to cost to arrive at the retail price for goods or services.

Net asset value: The value of an asset which is its original cost, less accumulated depreciation and liens.

Net profit (net income or net earnings):	Money remaining after deducting all operating expenses including taxes; gross profit minus operating expenses.
Net worth:	See the Book Value of a business (it's the same thing).
Note; promissory	A written promise to repay a loan. Usually a key part of a business sale. Normally written from the buyer to the seller for a period of 5–10 years.
Note receivable:	A debt that is evidenced by a note or other written acknowledgment.
Obsolescence:	Loss of value of a fixed asset arising because improved assets become available.
Operating cash flow:	This is cash flow directly generated by a business's operations. It's calculated by taking net income plus depreciation minus the increase in accounts receivable minus any increase in inventory plus any increase in accruals (money owned to the business as a result of operations). This is a mouthful to say but important to understand if you're going to underwrite a business expansion effort or anything else that requires cash flow generated by the business.
Operating income:	This is earnings (profit) before deduction of interest payments and income taxes. This is a very important number for a buyer and seller of a business to know because it's the basis for the ability of the business to repay debt. In almost every case involving the purchase of a small business, the buyer will in some way finance the purchase (bank, SBA, seller, family, etc.).
Overhead:	Method of allocating all non-labor costs to the various products manufactured or services performed.
Partner:	One of multiple owners of an unincorporated business.
Partnership:	A legal business association of two or more persons co-owning a business and sharing in the profits and losses. Although there are several kinds of partnerships, the two most common are; general and limited partnerships.

Patent:	A right to a process or a product granted to its inventor or the inventor's assignee for their exclusive use.
Physical inventory, taking of:	Counting all merchandise on hand, usually at the end of an accounting period.
Present value:	The value in current dollars of a future sum.
Profit:	The same as earnings and income.
Profit, gross:	Sales minus cost of goods sold.
Profit and Loss Statement:	The same as the Income and Expense Statement
Pro Forma:	A set of projected financial statements for a business which usually includes: Income and Expense Statements, Cash Flow Projections, and Balance Sheets. Generally, in a purchase and sale of a business, a seller prepares an optimistic Pro Forma Statement. The buyer should ensure that a realistic Pro Forma is used as part of the Business Plan for the newly acquired business.
Promissory Note:	A written promise to pay a sum of money at a specified future date in accordance with a pre-determined interest rate and payment schedule.
Proprietor:	The only owner of an unincorporated business who is responsible for its operation and liabilities.
Prorate:	Spread equally over a period of time.
Quick ratio:	The ratio of liquid assets to current liabilities. This is also known as the "acid test" ratio. If an operating business routinely has fewer liquid assets than its current liabilities, problems are sure to follow.
Receipts:	Sometimes used interchangeably with sales and revenue.
Residual value:	Estimated scrap or resale value of a tangible asset.
Return on investment:	The annual income that an investment earns. Usually expressed as a percentage relative to the purchase and sale of a business.

Revenue:	The gross income received as a result of business operations.
Sales:	Same as revenue.
Service business:	A firm dealing in non-merchandising activities.
SIC Code:	Standard Industrial Classification Code assigned to businesses within an industrial category as determined by the U.S. Department of Commerce.
Simple interest:	Interest on principal only, as compared to compound interest which is interest on both principal and accumulated interest.
Sole proprietorship:	A form of business owned by one person who is responsible for the entire business operations and liabilities.
Solvency:	Ability of a business to meet interest costs and repayment schedules associated with long-term obligations.
Subchapter S Corporation:	A small business corporation authorized by the IRS in which the owner(s) personally pay the corporation's income taxes.
Subsidiary operations:	The operations of a business that are separately accounted for in the financial statements. Usually used for ease of business operations through separate profit centers.
Sweat equity:	A slang term generally used to mean the value of a business over and above its net asset value. Also known as goodwill.
Stockholder:	An owner of an incorporated business, the ownership being evidenced by stock certificates.
Tangible asset:	A physical asset; a plant asset.
Taxable income:	Income on which income tax is computed; gross income minus both exemptions and personal deductions.
Trademark:	A legal right given by the U.S. Patent and Trademark Office for a name or symbol, granting its creator exclusive use.
Trade Name:	The business name under which a business operates. Sometimes known as the d/b/a (doing business as ...). Also referred to as the "fictitious name."

Turnover: The rate at which an asset is replaced within a given time period; usually refers to annual rate of replacement of stock (inventory turnover) or payment of accounts (accounts receivable turnover).

Venture capitalist: A person or entity with the purpose of investing funds in business startups, expansions, acquisitions, new products, etc., generally for the purpose of realizing financial returns through ownership of equity positions in the business.

Working capital: The readily convertible capital required in a business to permit the regular carrying forward of operations free from financial embarrassment. In accounting, the excess of current assets over current liabilities as of any date.

Write down: To reduce the book value of an asset to its current market value where the asset has actually decreased in value faster than it has been depreciated.

Yield: The return on one's investment, expressed as an annual rate of earnings as a percentage based on cost.

Reader Feedback Request

I'd really like to know what you thought of this book. I've tried very hard to present a complex and challenging undertaking in a clear, concise, and easy to understand format without overwhelming the reader.

I believe that I've covered all of the key information areas necessary to help buyers and sellers of profitable operating businesses find each other and relatively easily close the deal.

How did I do?

Your feedback to me will be greatly appreciated. Please, just jot down your thoughts about this book and mail, fax, or e-mail them to me at:

Mr. Russell L. Brown, *President and author*

The Business Book Press
RDS Associates, Inc.
41 Brainerd Road
Niantic, CT 06357
FAX: 860-691-1145   e-mail: rds@businessbookpress.com

I'll be sure to remember you with special consideration for future business information related publications!

_____

_____

_____

_____

_____

_____

_____

_____

Thanks!

Index

BizPricer™ Business Valuation Software

BizPricer™ is an absolutely superb, extremely cost-effective resource for prospective business buyers and sellers (and business brokers) who want to know the fair market value of a business! Includes an easy to understand manual that walks you through the valuation process and provides you with plenty of examples. The software accomplishes all of the calculations for you...all you do is enter the company's financial data.

No financial expertise or specialized knowledge is needed. Save hundreds to thousands of dollars over hiring an appraiser to provide you with a similar result. Use the software over and over again for "what-if" analysis as you negotiate. The software uses the same valuation method used by the author/business appraiser in hundreds of business valuations and verified against actual data and real-world results:

- **Business Buyers:** Estimate a solid fair market value for the business you're considering buying. Don't overpay for an over-valued business. Experience shows that many businesses are overpriced by at least 50% if the seller or business broker has set the price without a professional appraisal.

- **Business Sellers:** What's your business really worth? Don't leave money on the table! Find out now what your business might sell for in a fair market transaction and learn what factors may need to be increased to maximize the selling price.

- **Business Brokers:** Forget trying to figure out the fair market value of a business on the back of an envelope or by using expensive software that calculates dozens of different values using several different methods that have little relationship to the real world. Calculate an estimated fair market value for the business that makes sense for both buyers and sellers. Don't waste your time trying to market an overpriced business that won't stand up to a reasonable return on investment test.

We understand that every business situation is unique so....BizPricer™ includes a free quick-response E-mail hotline for questions users may have as they use the software. You'll never be alone. Answers to your questions will be only a mouse-click away!

A message from the author:

I've created BizPricer™ to be a straight-forward tool for business buyers and sellers to quickly estimate the fair market value of a business. No special knowledge of financial analysis or Microsoft Excel is needed. I've used the most commonly accepted method of valuing a business and eliminated all of the many other methods that lead to the same conclusion. I've kept the process as simple as possible without losing the ability to calculate a very accurate estimate of what the business will sell for. I've included a handy guide that not only walks you through the process, but provides you with specific examples from actual appraisals. If you can enter numbers (income a nd expenses for the business) into a table, then you can use BizPricer! And ... I've kept the price low enough that you can't afford not to use it. I'm pleased to be able to help in the process of bringing buyers and sellers together. As I say in my book, Strategies for Successfully Buying or Selling a Business, "the best deal is a fair deal."

Russell L. Brown

PC or MAC compatible. Requires the user to have Microsoft Excel™ software available on their computer. Shipped on CD-ROM (or Diskette available upon request). Only $99.95 plus $4.95 for Priority Mail shipping and handling. Please specify if Diskette is wanted. Otherwise ships as PC/MAC compatible CD-ROM.

RDS Associates, Inc. 41 Brainerd Road, Niantic, CT 06357 **www.BusinessBookPress.com**
or call toll free 1-800-363-8867 or Fax 1-860-691-1145 or e-mail rds@businessbookpress.com

Name_____

Address_____

City _____ State_____ Zip_____

Telephone # _____

Fax # _____

e-mail _____

☐ Please Charge to my: ☐ Check Enclosed

☐ MC   ☐ VISA   ☐ DISCOVER   ☐ AMEX

Account # ☐☐☐☐☐☐☐☐☐☐☐☐☐☐☐☐

Expiration Date_____

Signature _____

Item	Title			Total Price
S101	*BizPricer™ Business Valuation Software*			$99.95
	Shipping and Handling (Priority Mail)			4.95
			SUBTOTAL	104.90
	CT residents only, please add 6% sales tax		CT SALES TAX*	
			TOTAL	

Member of the Connecticut Better Business Bureau

The Business Reference Guide

12th Edition, 725 pages, paperback

This professional reference guide is loaded with information for business brokers, mergers and acquisition specialists, appraisers, accountants and business intermediaries of all kinds. This "behind the scenes" collection of key information and insiders secrets is not readily available outside of the business brokerage industry.

If you're contemplating buying, selling, or determining the value of a business and you want the information these professionals use, then this book is for you! As a business buyer or seller, you'll have hundreds of thousands, perhaps millions of dollars at stake in the transaction. You owe it to your financial well-being and peace of mind to have all the information you can get!

With this "bible" of the business brokerage world you'll learn how to ensure that your particular deal makes absolute sense. You'll also fully understand what the business broker is (or should be) doing for you, whether you're a buyer or seller.

The book is professionally edited and soft-cover bound. An extensive table of contents and index allows you to easily find the specific information you need.

Kiplinger's Personal Finance Magazine has described this book as "a GOLD MINE of information which includes profiles of many businesses and guides to legal, pricing, and financial issues." Inc. Magazine has also highly recommended this book to their readers who are considering buying or selling a business!

Special features include:

- An impressive listing of over 500 rules of thumb for "ballpark" valuing over 100 different businesses. The best published set of rules of thumb available!

- A superb collection of professional resources (including individuals, firms, organizations, publications and software, for every facet of the business buying, selling and valuation process.

This book is NOT available in bookstores or through on-line book sellers like Amazon. Please order your copy from the Business Book Press now!

To learn more about this publication and to order online please visit:

http://www.BusinessBookPress.com

Or call us at **800-363-8867**

Or use the order blank on the reverse side of this page to order by postal mail or fax.

ORDER FORM

"Strategies for Successfully Buying or Selling a Business"
OR
"Preparing Your Business For Sale"
OR
"The Business Reference Guide"

- Fax Orders: (860) 691-1145
- Telephone Orders: 1-800-363-8867
- E-mail Orders: rds@businessbookpress.com
- Mail Orders: RDS Associates, Inc./Business Book Press
                      41 Brainerd Road, Niantic, Connecticut 06357

☐ Please send_____ copies of *"Strategies For Successfully Buying Or Selling A Business"* at $49.95/each

☐ Please send_____ copies of *"Preparing Your Business For Sale"* at $49.95/each

☐ Please send_____ copies of *"The Business Reference Guide"* at $88.00/each

☐ **Please send me a FREE catalog of your other great business book titles**

Company Name: _____

Name:_____

Address: _____

City _____ State _____ Zip _____

Sales Tax: Connecticut residents please add 6% sales tax for each book

Shipping: $4.95 for the first book (sent by priority mail), plus $2.00 for each additional book

Method of Payment:

☐ Check Enclosed   ☐ Visa   ☐ MasterCard   ☐ Discover   ☐ AMEX

Card Number_____ Exp Date _____

Name _____

Signature _____ Date _____

Visit us on the Internet for even more information and software resources to help you buy, sell or value a business: http://www.BusinessBookPress.com